Astral Projection for Beginners

How to Unlock Astral Travel, Bilocation, Lucid Dreaming, Extrasensory Perception, and Have Out-of-Body Experiences Using Safe Techniques - Guided Meditation Hypnosis Made Easy

Bodhi Fox

2021 All rights reserved. This book or parts thereof may not be reproduced in any form, stored in any retrieval system, or transmitted in any form by any means—electronic, mechanical, photocopy, recording, or otherwise—without prior written permission of the publisher, except as provided by United States of America copyright law. For permission requests, write to the publisher, at "Attention: Permissions Coordinator," at the address below.

Table of Contents

Introduction

Part 1: Astral Travel, Out of Body Experiences and Bilocation

Section 1: Understanding Astral Travel and Out of Body Experiences
When You Leave Your Body
Maintaining Peace and Harmony in the Dimensions

Section 2: How to Astral Travel
Techniques to Help You Start an Astral Journey

Section 3: Bilocation Technique for Beginners
What is Bilocation?
Invert Your Corridor of Light

Section 4: Out of Body Experiences or OBE's
The Natural Ability to have an OBE since Childhood

Section 5: Various Planes of Existence

Section 6: Astral Projection and Food
What Are Real Foods?
What to Eat
Foods to Avoid if You Want to Astral Travel
Other Toxins

Part Two: Lucid Dreaming

Section 1: What is Lucid Dreaming?

Section 2: How to Improve Your Awareness
Short-Term Goals
Long-Term Goals

Section 3: Lucid Dreaming: The History and Timeline

Section 4: How to Keep an Accurate Dream Journal
The Step-by-Step Guide to a Successful Dream Journal
What to Include in Your Template

Section 5: Lucid Dreaming Stories

Section 6: What Are the Dangers of Lucid Dreaming?
How to Manage Your Fears During Lucid Dreaming

Section 7: Hypnagogic Exercises
Exercise to Help You Develop Control

Section 8: Mnemonic Induced Lucid Dreaming (MILD)
Common Mnemonics

Section 9: How to Get the Best Out of Your Lucid Dreams
The Power of Flight
Here's How to Prep for Your Dreamy Encounter
Embrace the Magic of Dreams

Section 10: Lucid Tech

Part Three: Extra Sensory Perception

Section 1: The History of ESP
The Symbols

Section 2: Signs That You Have ESP

Section 3: Clairaudience
9 Signs That You Are Clairaudient
How to Develop Your Ability to Communicate Using Clairaudience

Section 4: Clairvoyance
Famous Clairvoyants in History

    How to Tell if You Have the Power of Clairvoyance
    Additional Signs of Clairvoyance
    Exercises to Improve Your Clairvoyance Skills

Section 5: Mediums
    Signs That You Are a Natural Medium

Section 6: Precognition
    Signs You Have the Gift of Precognition
    Types of Precognitive Abilities
    Precognitive Dreaming
    What to Do to Heighten Your Precognition Skills

Section 7: Psychometry
    The Best Items for Psychometry
    A Basic Exercise for Beginners

Section 8: Psychic Detectives

Section 9: Remote Viewing
    How Do I Practice Remote Viewing?
    Are All Remote Viewings the Same?

Section 10: Retrocognition
    Signs That You Have Retrocognition Abilities
    True Tales of Retrocognition
    How to Develop Your Retrocognition Skills

Section 11: Telekinesis
    What Is the Energy Used in Telekinesis?
    How to Practice Telekinesis
    Here are Some Advanced Exercises for You to Try

Section 12: Telepathy
    Type 1: Instinctual Telepathy

Type 2: Animal Telepathy
Type 3: Mental Telepathy
Type 4: Spiritual Telepathy
Signs That You Have Telepathic Abilities

Part 4: Guided Meditation
The Move from a Safe Place to a Brave Space
Prepare Yourself for Sleep Meditation
The Loving Kindness Meditation

Conclusion

References

Part 1: Astral Travel, Out of Body Experiences and Bilocation

What are the astral realms or dimensions, and why would you want to visit them? Because you can? Because you feel restricted by earthly limitations, or you simply need to know what is out there. All these reasons are perfectly valid, and there are thousands more to consider. We all have emotions and reactions to physical experiences, so why wouldn't we want to visit somewhere more spiritual in order to heal?

Whatever your reasons, the techniques in this section will help you attain your dreams and enable you to travel through astral planes.

Section 1: Understanding Astral Travel and Out of Body Experiences

We live in a multi-dimensional world, and how we explore it is limited by our physical bodies. The realms that exist outside of our physical beings are only reached by setting our minds free and roaming without the shackles of our physical self. This is known as astral traveling and is one way we can visit the fractal elements that exist in our consciousness. Out-of-body experiences are the same form of traveling but are credited with less spiritual intent.

Different dimensions and planes have different sets of rules which are apparent when you visit. Some dimensions are physical and bear a resemblance to our Earth, while others have ethereal qualities that mean they exist in a form that is alien to us. Don't let that put you off. Astral travel is all about the experience and learning to grow.

Different beings exist within these dimensions, and they all live in varying ways. You will receive feedback from each of your journeys that can be collected and studied to help your spiritual growth. If you aren't particularly spiritual, you will benefit from the wisdom and love you will experience. You will learn new skills and abilities that you can utilize on Earth.

Some realms are there solely for your self-help. They can work with you to reduce fear and anxieties and quieten the mental clamor that may be messing with your perception. The beings who work with you recognize that you intend to travel the astral planes, but your mental issues are preventing you from attaining your dream.

When You Leave Your Body

In the astral realm, you will experience a bigger reality. It will feel real because your intent determines it. You are part of the universe, and it is your perception that will guide you. If you meet someone else when you are traveling, they have their own out-of-body experience, and it will seem like a "normal" meeting. How you both remember it when you are conscious will differ because of your personal mind filters.

Time doesn't exist in astral realms. You are in a dimension that you have created so you can decide what happens. You may feel like you have been there for minutes, or it can feel like hours or days. There are some quirky ways to travel once you've mastered the basic techniques, and you can have fun with your choices. Just like the "get lucky" button on Google, you can intend the same concept for your traveling. Ask the universe to direct you to a random dimension and sit back and enjoy the ride.

Some people experience more formal experiences within the dimensions. They have been set tests while they are in the astral zone that determines how much they have learned. Some people are set tasks and must mentally manifest the solution to these tasks. For instance, if the universe sets a scenario where you are a chef in a restaurant and have 120 orders for food, it will instruct your mind to manifest the food to feed all the customers. Sometimes these tests will involve moral dilemmas and ask how you would deal with situations. If you pass these tests, you will be granted access to sources of knowledge and power.

You may feel cheated by these sorts of tests and wonder why you have been singled out. The truth is, you will only be tested if your subconscious asks to be. Remember, everything that happens to you in the astral realm is based on your own intentions and is sent to benefit you. Some people believe that the ultimate form of tests is classed as alien abduction. Would you let aliens experiment on you if you thought it would help them? Remember, you have the right to say no to any experience, and you should trust your integrity to lead you to the right solution.

Out-of-body experiences differ slightly as they involve more direct contact with the physical world. You can have conversations with people on the physical plane that they may hear even when they can't see you. You can visit other physical environments and travel with speed between your chosen destinations. Energy balls can be used to move physical objects and teleport them through physical spaces. You can't bring non-physical objects into the physical plane, as they won't be able to maintain their form.

Mana

Finding the right path is all about mana. This is the spiritual power we all have, and adding to it will help you develop into a more aware being. You can learn from the universe how to accomplish things and improve your intent. The ultimate goal is to become an enlightened being who can go on and teach others. There are multiple opportunities to learn in the astral realm, and you can find the answers to all your questions. Schools and temples are designed to teach you about relationships, sex, physical and mental health, self-development, how the universe works, etc.

Once you have reached a certain level of mana, you can become a teacher. Everything you can imagine can be taught in the astral zone. Teach people how to improve their astral travel skills or share your meditation tips. Whatever you feel are your strengths, you will have the opportunity to share with others.

Section 2: How to Astral Travel

Before you begin your journey, you need to prepare for what you are about to do. Create positive affirmations to prepare your mind and body for astral projection. "I can have astral journeys," or "I want to expand my mind and visit other dimensions," or "My mind is my strongest muscle, and I need to flex it" will focus your mind on your intent.

Join like-minded groups and share your stories and expectations with them. When you talk to other enthusiasts, you will find different methods and techniques that will help you expand your knowledge. Sometimes it can feel like you're the only person who believes in such a phenomenon where, in reality, the world is filled with believers and practitioners.

When you first start to travel, the experience can become overwhelming. The excitement you feel can work against you and shake you out of the experience. Calm your mind and take anything that happens in your stride. There will be strange noises and vibrations as you leave your body, so ask your spiritual guides to protect you. Nothing will harm you, and you are always going to be safe.

Techniques to Help You Start an Astral Journey

Set Your Intentions

Never forget that you are in charge, so remember to set your intentions and tell the universe what you want.

Relax

You need to be relaxed in both mind and body. There are some guided meditations in this book that can help you. Lying on your back with your hands on top of your stomach and chest will help you heal any anxiety and stress. Clear your mind and embrace the calm.

Lying still in a frozen position is also recommended. Stay perfectly still and wait for the natural vibrations of your body to kick in. Imagine you have been struck by lightning and feel the energy from the bolt flood your body. Once you feel energized, imagine turning your head around with your mind. Put your head where your legs are, and put your legs where your head is.

Prepare to Depart from Your Body

Make your mind enter a hypnotic state that is somewhere in between sleep and lucidity. You should begin to see lights and orbs begin to form on your close eyelids that weave and capture your attention. Now let your mind move to your foot and imagine moving it within your astral force field. Try the same thing with other parts of your body until you become to feel detached. Keep your focus, and you should be able to move all the parts of your body with ease.

At this stage, you will feel vibrations that can be disturbing for beginners. Don't worry. They are part of the meditative state and signal that you are ready to begin your journey for real.

The Rope Technique

If this is your first journey or you are still feeling unsure about your abilities, try the rope technique to give you an extra push to leave your body. This is the point where you can exert your control and master your willpower. In your mind, imagine a rope descending from the heavens and hanging right in front of you. Without opening your eyes or moving any part of your physical self, reach out and place your hands on the bottom of the rope.

Once you can feel the physical sense of the rope, lower your hands and bring them back to your physical self. Let the vibrations slow down and return to a calm state. If you still feel you are in a hypnotic state, you can try the technique again. Wait for the vibrations to resume and control them with your mind.

Reach for the rope and grasp it again, but this time, hold on tight. Raise your body by moving your hands up the rope as you rise. Place one hand over your other hand as if you were pulling yourself up in real life. The vibrations will buzz at a higher frequency as you make your way up the rope, and they can be disturbing. If you feel overwhelmed, you can return to your body and try the technique again later.

If you can get past the high frequencies, concentrate on your quest and keep climbing. Don't stop until you feel that satisfying feeling of your spiritual self fully separating from your physical self.

The Silver Cord Technique

Once you have mastered the rope technique, you will find separation from your physical body easy to master. Now you need to use a technique that keeps you connected to your physical body and makes sure you are safe. This is known as the silver cord and is the life thread that connects the higher self to the physical body. Some people describe it as the spiritual form of the umbilical cord that feeds you and keeps you alive.

However, when it comes to the connection concept of the cord, it goes far beyond feeding and growth. The cord represents the link between the spirits of the mother and child. In the same way, the silver cord is the link between your spiritual soul and your physical self.

What Does the Cord Look Like?

Here's a weird fact. Most astral travelers know about the silver cord, and they recognize the part it plays in astral traveling, but they don't ever see it. Most regular travelers report they "feel separate yet connected" from their body and are aware of an energy connection between the two states of being. The most common reports of visual sightings of a silver cord are when individuals experience near-death experiences. This is probably why some people fear astral travel as they connect it with death.

People who report seeing a silver cord describe it as an inch wide silver cord that looks like a tinsel. Some individuals say it has an elastic quality, and it buzzes with energy. It is connected to the back of the spiritual form, which allows the soul to travel forward while remaining connected. The intent behind the journey will determine the position - it will be attached to the head if the focus is mental and at the heart if the focus is more emotional. Some people have described the cord protruding from their back to connect with the physical form.

What Happens When the Silver Cord is Broken?

When the cord breaks, you die. Should this worry you? No, it shouldn't. The cord isn't easily broken, and it can only be severed when the physical body dies on the earthly plane.

Imagine you have a heart attack, and your soul begins to rise from your body in readiness for your death. Your astral body will begin to move away, but the cord still holds you. If you are revived during this period, the cord will help you return to your physical self and return to consciousness. If the cord breaks, you will die and continue your journey as a departed soul.

This theory is supported by people who have had near-death experiences and witnessed their astral beings hovering over their physical selves attached by a silver cord.

Explore the Plane

Once you have left your body, explore your physical plane before other dimensions. Leave the room your body is in and travel through to another room. Make a note of the objects in that room and the details of what you can see. When you return to your physical body, check the room you visited and see if the details correspond to the actual room and objects.

Now you can leave your body and project yourself into the astral realms. Enjoy your newfound skills and embrace the experiences you are about to have.

Section 3: Bilocation Technique for Beginners

What is Bilocation?

This is another form of astral travel that involves splitting your energy. You travel to different planes, but you leave residual parts of your body in the physical plane. Historical evidence of bilocation is well documented and often involved saints and other revered beings appearing in two different locations simultaneously.

On a personal level, people who bilocate prefer this method as it allows them to remain anchored in the physical world and lessens the risk of becoming detached from reality.

We will explore two different types of relocation exercises that involve external and internal forms of bilocation. Try them both and experience the mirror effect of both techniques.

Traveling Through the Light Corridor

As we already know, the main point of the experience is your chosen destination. Your intent is fueling the journey, so it should be your starting point. Do you feel a pull from one of the traditional spiritual planes, or do you require a more personal destination? If you regularly require some form of spiritual healing, you can create a healing room to visit and fill it with all the tools you need.

Your healing room can be as simple or as complex as you like. It can be a fantasy world filled with a healing team from another planet who have skills way beyond our limitations, or it can be a place where your spirit guides can heal you with love and wisdom. Create your space with intent. Picture how it looks and feels from the interior and who is there waiting for you.

Maybe you prefer to visit more ethereal worlds, filled with spiritual beings who can welcome you in and make you feel special. Perhaps the physical world is more appealing. Have you always wanted to visit the summit of Everest or the middle of the Atlantic? Remember that astral traveling has no boundaries or limitations, and you can go wherever you want.

Once You Have Your Destination in Mind, It's Time to Start the Journey

Stage 1: Enter a State of Meditation that Suits Your Intention

You can use the guided meditations in this book or just relax with simple breathing techniques. Focus on an object in your eye-line and control your breaths. Take deep breaths and exhale for five minutes until you feel your mind start to relax. Picture the destination you have chosen and create a corridor of light. You can ask your spirit guides to help you achieve this, or you can use your own power of intention.

Stage 2: Begin to Travel

Once the corridor appears, step into it and begin to spiral up as the energy fills your body. You will consciously choose a part of your energy to remain on Earth as the remaining part of you rises through the dimensions. You will feel your vibrations rise as the light envelops you. Once your frequency matches the one in the corridor, it's time to step out to the other side.

Stage 3: Explore

Once you reach your destination, it's time to explore. If you are in your healing room, lie down on the healing beds and let your teamwork on you. This is a safe space where you can regenerate and repair. Trust these people to have your back. They are an extension of your inner psyche, so they have your best interests at heart. Ask whatever you want and state whatever you need.

If you have chosen a more traditional destination, take your time to explore and see the sights. You may be able to interact with locals, or you can choose to wander about without causing any effect. Remember, this is your experience, and you set the intent.

Stage 4: Return to Your Physical Self

Once you decide to return to your body, the corridor will appear. Step into it and feel the pull of your physical self-propel you back to Earth. The return journey is the perfect time to realign your body and mind. When you reach the remaining physical part of yourself, make sure you align completely and become a stronger being than the person you were before.

Invert Your Corridor of Light

When you are just starting out, astral travel can seem daunting. Projecting yourself into other dimensions will feel unnatural and strange for beginners. Inverting your journey helps you to become adjusted to astral traveling, and you know what to expect.

Stage 1: Choose Your Destination

Just like regular astral travel, you need to set your intention. Choose an internal part of your body to visit. The most powerful inner realm is your heart, and there is a wormhole there that can lead to further exploration. Choose the chakra that suits your needs and create the intention to visit there.

The Seven Chakras and What They Mean

- The first chakra is the root chakra and is situated in the coccyx area.

- The second is the sacral chakra and is in the lower belly just under the naval.

- The third is the solar plexus chakra and is located just below the heart.

- The fourth is the heart chakra and is located in the chest.

- The fifth is the throat chakra and is located in the neck area at the carotid plexus.

- The sixth is the third eye chakra which is located between the eyebrows.

- The seventh is the crown chakra located at the top of the cranium.

These are the subtle energies that govern our lives. They are the crossroads that bind the material with the immaterial and the source of all our spiritual and physical spirits. When we get blockages in our chakras, it affects us both physically and spiritually. Internal bilocation will help you clear any blockages and benefit from the energies.

Stage 2: Build Your Bridge

You can use the corridor of light method, or you could choose another method. A bridge that leads to the inner realms of your heart will feel like a solid way to reach your destination. Simply walk along the bridge to gain access to your heart chakra, where the natural vibrations will help filter out any unwanted energies.

Stage 3: Explore

The heart chakra is the perfect point to begin your journey. You can travel upward to the higher chakras or downward to your lower energy sources. The heart chakra becomes your base camp where you can re-energize and regroup. Once you feel like you have completed your explorations, it's time to return home.

Stage 4: Return

Take the same route home to your remaining physical sense that you took to your internal destinations. As you enter the corridor or take your first steps on your bridge, prepare yourself for realignment by studying how you have become stronger and healthier.

Section 4: Out of Body Experiences or OBE's

Astral projecting is a spiritual event and involves the soul connection and spiritual encounters. This form of traveling is more likely to be described as part of the paranormal phenomenon, while OBEs are not at all paranormal. They can happen to anybody, and there are no links to spirituality or belief in higher beings. OBEs tend to be earth-based and rarely involve more astral journeys.

There have been multiple case studies involving individuals who claim to have the power to leave their bodies at will. This has led researchers to consider if having an OBE is a skill we all have, but we have lost the ability over time. Occurrences in children are more prevalent than in adults, which suggests that it is an inherent ability that fades with age. Some individuals have reported cases of OBE.

The Natural Ability to have an OBE since Childhood

In 2014, the University of Ottawa funded research into OBE's that involved studying the brain activity of a student at the University who claimed she could leave her body at will. The woman claimed she had been leaving her physical body since an early age, and her first recollections were associated with sleep time in preschool. She claimed that while her classmates slept, she would leave her physical body and roam around the school.

It wasn't until she attended a lecture about OBE's that she realized that other people couldn't leave their bodies at will. After consulting with her lecturer, tests were conducted on her brain during her self-induced OBE. The scans showed that the woman's visual cortex was disabled, and all her brain activity was restricted to the left side of her brain.

The visual cortex is normally activated when we imagine things in our heads, and during imaginary scenarios, most people use both sides of their brain. These deviations were unexplainable and only occurred during periods of OBE.

The woman explained that she often found it difficult to sleep without her regular OBE in her life. She described the sensation of separation as soothing and described how she enjoyed the accompanying vibrations. She described the process of separation as moving away from her physical self and rotating around the space above her physical self. She told the researchers that she felt no duality with her body and considered her mental form to be the active part of her being. The body that lay below her was forgotten as she concentrated on moving her non-corporeal self around her environment.

The studies concluded that more subjects need to be studied before a conclusive interpretation can be reached.

Eugene

In Nepal, a 36-year-old man turned to meditation to deal with his stress, which led to him having regular OBE experiences. He attended a lecture on mindfulness in a local meditation center and found that his experiences were being talked about. After approaching the lecturer, Eugene agreed to test his newfound ability with the room. He handed out post-it notes to several of the people in the room and told them to write a number between 1 and 100 on each note. He asked them to place the notes face up on the floor while he left the room and underwent an OBE and was "gone." They did as he asked, and after a short period, they picked them up and put them out of sight. When Eugene returned to the room, he correctly identified all the numbers written on the notes.

Anna

When she was 14, Anna had a dream that she was in her grandparent's kitchen when her grandma turned to her grandad and complained of chest pains. She witnessed her grandad in tears and her grandma trying to comfort him. Anna woke in tears and felt an overpowering feeling of loss and grief. She put the experience behind her and carried on with her normal day.

A couple of days later, Anna's grandad phoned the home to tell the family that his wife, Anna's grandma, had died from a massive heart attack while she was in the kitchen. Anna traveled with her family to their grandparents' home, where they had moved less than a year before. Despite never having been there before, Anna recognized the kitchen as the scene from her dream.

She kept her secret until 15 years later when she confided to her mother what she had dreamed about just before her grandmother's death. Her mother wasn't surprised at her revelation, as she knew Anna and her grandfather were close. Anna believes that she traveled to the future to witness her grandma's death because of the closeness she had with them both. It made her realize that the bonds that tie us to others go way beyond physical boundaries.

These are just a few stories of OBE's and how they have affected people's lives. Some can be dismissed as trickery and some form of deceit, while others are harder to explain. Surely young children and teens have no reason to lie or exaggerate their experiences. There are multiple studies and research into the subject, which can only lead to more understanding of why we have this ability.

Section 5: Various Planes of Existence

In Sanskrit and Buddhism, there are 31 realms of existence, but more traditional beliefs have just 11 or 7 depending on which belief system you follow.

These Are the 11 Planes That Cover Existence as We Know It

1) **The physical plane:** This is our earthly plane where we use our regular senses - we hear, taste, smell, touch, and see what is right in front of us. Magic is here and can be used with the ability to access it.

2) **The mental plane:** This is the existence where thoughts and mind-stuff are found. There are no physical beings on this plane, and it is formed purely by existential thoughts and ideas. This plane is the source of telekinesis and telepathy. This is a realm that encourages you to indulge in yourself and your wildest fantasies.

3) **The love plane:** This form of existence is only reached by making love or having orgasmic sex. In some cultures, women were worshipped because they could take men to this plane of existence with their bodies and minds. Today we prefer to believe that this plane is more accessible to couples who have become so entwined in each other they have reached true love.

4) **The ghostly plane:** This is the place where spirits rest before they enter the Afterlife. The location will seem familiar, so the spirit can contemplate their situation before leaving familiar things behind.

5) **The evil plane:** Also referred to as the Underworld, this is a dark and dangerous place. It is often depicted as a dark, dank cave that is deep underground and guarded by demons. The force of darkness rules this realm.

6) **The good plane:** This is the place where morality and good magic reside. When our mortal souls get to this plane, they are given a choice to choose between right and wrong. If you are facing a mental dilemma, you may find yourself on this plane to face your options.

7) **The ethereal plane:** This is a plane where gravity doesn't exist. It rests in between the physical plane and the astral plane and is a sparse wasteland. The weather is constant and unmoving. Here meteorology becomes geography.

8) **The causal plane:** Not much is known about this plane as it is situated beyond the astral plane and is rarely visited by lesser mortals. Some faiths believe this is where deities dwell.

9) **The cosmic plane:** This is the realm of the Fates and the Angels of Destiny. The beings that live here are responsible for the universe and all it contains. They mapped the stars and placed the planets in the cosmos.

10) **The spiritual plane:** Also known as the Afterlife. Spirits that make this plane their home have chosen to become guides to earthly beings. They have passed on but are content to keep their ties with mortals. Guardian angels and spiritual guides form a vanguard to watch over earthly beings. They can be summoned with a simple spell or spiritual connection.

11) **The astral plane:** This is the place where the souls of the vanquished reside. It is visually hard to imagine as the surface has the qualities of plasma, and everything is super bright and vivid. There are two levels of the astral plane, which consist of upper and lower levels. The souls of demons and wrongdoers are sent to the lower plane, frozen in time, a place described as a wasteland for the soul. Very few beings can visit this level and survive. An

upper level is a plane where all souls visit before progressing to the physical plane to live their mortal life.

The omniverse is a subject that has many theories and conjectures surrounding it. Different beliefs will place the planes in varying orders, and the journey through the planes will differ. Science has developed various theories about super dimensionality and the membranes that divide them. They have discovered wormholes and black holes that could lead to the possibility of parallel worlds and mirroring dimensions.

The boundaries of our five senses restrict scientific investigations, but other fields can see beyond these restrictions. They understand that true astral travel involves using all our abilities and refusing to be bound by conventions. They believe that the levels of existence could be limitless and continue to develop as humans embrace the concept and begin to travel within them.

Section 6: Astral Projection and Food

Does food affect your ability to astral travel or have out-of-body experiences?

When you consider how the phenomenon of astral traveling has been documented through the ages, it would seem it doesn't. How can the ancient Egyptians, Aztec shamans, and Celtic druids have a common diet? How can all cultures who have connections with astral travel be eating the same food?

The truth is that it's not particular foods that help you to astral travel. It is some basic detail about your diet that matters. You need to have a healthy diet that includes real food, just like your ancestors did. The modern world is filled with food that has been designed to look appealing. Yet, they are basically chemical compounds designed to look and taste like food, but they have extraordinarily little nutritional value.

Another myth about diet and astral traveling is that meat-eaters are excluded. Some people have stated that astral projection and spiritual traveling are only possible for vegetarians. While meat is harder to process and requires more energy, consider the Inuit people. They lived in extremely harsh environments and existed on a diet of meat and fat with truly little opportunity to have fruit and veg. Despite this, their culture and faith have numerous references to astral travel and the ability to journey to celestial places.

What Are Real Foods?

Hopefully, we all know what real food means. Here are some points of clarification to make sure all the food you eat is "real":

- If a single item of food has more than five ingredients, it isn't real food.
- Ingredient lists overall are a strong indication it isn't real food.

- When you compare the ingredients to the finished item, it has no resemblance.
- Imagine traveling back in time and giving it to your grandma to cook. What would she do? If she would throw it in the bin or be disturbed by it, it isn't real food.
- Leave it in the garden and see if the wildlife will eat it. Fun fact, even pigeons won't eat Quorn or tofu, and they regularly eat dog poop!

The fact of the matter is, if you are already eating for health and vitality, your diet is suitable for astral traveling. Once you focus on your intention to stay healthy, your body will start to crave these types of foods, and your abilities will improve. There are no specific foods that improve spiritual growth. Food can be healthy for the body yet harmful for the mind. An overall focus on what your body is telling you will help you eat well and grow spiritually in the process.

What to Eat

Vegetables

It may seem like a cliché, but the five portions a day rule is a great start to a healthy diet. It is the minimum requirement for healthy living, and you should build on this foundation.

Focus on cruciferous vegetables like kale and spinach. Add broccoli and beetroot to boost your iron levels, especially if you are following a vegan diet. If you are adventurous with your diet, try sea vegetables to make your diet more interesting and benefit from the healthy ingredients.

Sea Vegetables

- **Arame** is a brown algae used mainly in Japanese cooking. It's available in dried form all year round and can be added to most recipes and dishes. It is a natural detoxifier and will help cleanse your body of toxins and chemicals.

- **Dulse** has a smoky flavor and can be eaten as a healthy snack. It has a vast array of minerals and vitamins combined with protein and fiber that help your body benefit from the nutritional content. Add to a soup or sandwich to enhance the flavor.

- **Wakame** is an edible seaweed that is promoted as a tried and tested weight loss aid. Add it to your salads and benefit from the mineral content as well as vitamins A, B2, C, D, and K.

- **Nori** is possibly the best-known sea vegetable in the Western world. It is a red seaweed that can form sheets to wrap sushi in and is delicious when toasted. It's loaded with vitamins and minerals and tastes great.

- **Kombu** is a form of kelp that grows in shallow ocean waters. The plants form underground forests that can reach from the seafloor to the surface of the ocean. Kelp is packed with iodine and can be eaten in soups or stews or drunk as tea.

- **Agar** is a sweet version of algae. It has a jelly-like texture and can be used as a sugar substitute for dessert recipes. It has no carbs, fat, or sugar, yet it tastes delicious, especially if you have a sweet tooth.

- **Spirulina** is a blue-green algae mostly found in smoothies. In the wild, it can be found growing naturally on the top of ponds and is colloquially known as "pond scum" and dismissed by most people. It has been proclaimed as one of the best foods for the future and has been added to astronaut's diet plans by NASA.

Water

Staying hydrated is so important to your health, but few people make an effort to stay hydrated. Make sure the last thing you have before you go to bed is a glass of water. Flushing out toxins is essential for a healthy mental attitude and improves your ability to travel in an astral form. Adding lemon juice and kosher salt helps your drink to replace vitamin C and electrolytes so your body can function properly.

Proteins

Fish, eggs, dairy, and meats can be consumed in moderation. When you eat your food is also a major factor when you are eating healthy. The rule of thumb for an astral diet is to eat protein that is harder to digest on days when you don't plan to travel.

Fats

Stick to healthy organic fats and substitute your regular oils with coconut and avocado oil. They are better for cooking with, and they add taste to your food. Butter made from nuts is far healthier than animal-based alternatives, but it can be boring. Use discretion and have the dairy version as a treat.

Fruit

Although it is healthy and delicious, it can interfere with your astral journeys as it causes sugar spikes.

Carbohydrates

These are fine in moderation but try to stick to brown carbs whenever possible. Brown rice, bread, oat bran, or whole wheat will burn slower and give you energy for longer.

Foods to Avoid if You Want to Astral Travel

If you've ever been tested for food intolerance, you know the importance of knowing how certain items affect your body. If you are having trouble traveling or having other experiences, it could be your diet.

Alcohol should be avoided on the day you want to travel and the day before. Minimize your intake to keep your body more alert and less liable to fall asleep. Meditation is a key part of your experience, and when it is combined with alcohol, it can make you drowsy.

Coffee is also an irritant, and if you are agitated and tense, you are less likely to project. If you are a heavy caffeine user, just cut down gradually as the side effects can be unpleasant. Use decaffeinated coffee to reduce the effects it has on your sleep.

Sugar is perhaps the biggest culprit for preventing successful travel. If you need further proof, just watch kids who are hyped up on sugar. This is not how you want to be during your astral journeys.

Processed foods are an obvious no-no. Just refer to the section above about real food if you need more proof.

Smoking affects one of the central pillars of your health, your breathing. You need to be able to control the quality of the air you breathe at all times, and smoking doesn't let you do that. A smoker's cough will destroy any peaceful aspects of even the strongest meditation.

Other Toxins

Toxins surround us, and they aren't just in our food. We wash our clothes and clean our homes with more chemicals than ever before. Try using more organic compounds and cut down your exposure to harmful toxins. Before you apply any form of cream or lotion to your body, consider if there is a healthier version available.

We can't live in a bubble, but we can raise our awareness levels. If you are serious about any form of spiritual communication or traveling, you need to be more mindful.

You should also consider how much time you spend being exposed to harmful light forms both in your home and when at work. Electromagnetic fields and light pollution are two of the most harmful components when it comes to your health. Cut back on the time you spend in front of screens or artificially lit places.

The main point to take away from this section is not to obsess. You can still astral travel with bad habits, it's just more difficult. You could make it more difficult by going too far in the opposite direction. If you become obsessed with what is around you and the harm it can do, you will find it hard to focus properly.

Healthy food and spiritual growth are connected, but there is no such thing as an "astral diet" - just eat better and avoid unhealthy ingredients, simple, right?

Part Two: Lucid Dreaming

Section 1: What is Lucid Dreaming?

A lucid dream is any dream that leads to you becoming aware that you are dreaming. Your waking consciousness doesn't have any effect during regular dreams, but lucidity changes all that. When you are conscious of your dream, you can take some form of control over what happens.

When you trigger your waking consciousness in your sleep, you can do really cool things that are impossible in the real world:

- You can heighten your senses within your dreamscape. Your vision will be clearer, and everything you touch, hear, smell, or taste will blow your mind.

- Fantasy becomes a reality. Lucid dreaming opens possibilities that are out of this world. You aren't subject to regular constrictions, and your imagination can run riot.

- You can overcome your deepest fears. Do you have psychological issues that stop you from doing things in real life? Use your lucid dreaming experiences to overcome phobias and fears by facing them full-on. You know you are dreaming so you can be as brave as you like.

- Discover your inner creativity: Emulate the most creative people you know. Write songs or books that immediately become bestsellers or use your dreamscape to paint the masterpiece that lies within. There are no barriers, and you can create whatever you like.

Experts agree we all have the potential to lucid dream, yet very few of us do.

There is no doubt that lucid dreaming has been proved scientifically. Back in the 1970s, British researchers established contact with someone who was fully asleep. They recorded ocular signs that the subject was lucid dreaming and had full awareness of what was happening as they slept.

Further studies mean there is an abundance of scientific proof that lucid dreaming isn't just fun to do but can also be used to interact with your inner psyche. During lucid dreams, you can create a character that represents your co-conscious self and has in-depth conversations.

Psychologists have been using the process to help veterans recover from PTSD and cure children of their phobias. Sports experts have used lucid dreams to help athletes become better prepared for competitions.

We will discover the importance of self-awareness, dream recall, and reality checks in the sections ahead. We will uncover the most effective ways of inducing lucid dreams and how to get the best experiences possible. Some people fear the loss of control when you allow the subconscious to take charge, so we will also cover the truth about the potential dangers of lucid dreaming.

Perhaps the most pertinent thing about lucid dreaming is that it has been described as the perfect springboard for astral projecting, out-of-body experiences, and other forms of travel that involve the psyche.

Section 2: How to Improve Your Awareness

Your lucid dreaming techniques will work better if you are fully self-aware. You need to have a positive attitude and the ability to embrace all the experiences you will encounter. This form of self-improvement isn't just about dreaming; it's about your life. Becoming a whole individual should be something we all aspire to. No matter how self-confident you already are, there is always room for further growth. If you can work on your self-awareness, all your experiences will benefit from the process.

Do you drift through your day without being influenced by others? Are you in a self-built bubble designed to protect you from the world? That's all well and good, but it is harder for you to become involved in your dreams when you are closed off during the day. You will be relegated to being the eternal bystander and fail to experience the amazing world of lucid dreaming.

Awareness or consciousness is the minds' ability to take information from the external environment and process it to make decisions. Emotional influences and judgments need to be applied to factual choices and allow the mind to make clear and conscious decisions.

Awareness is the key to inner knowledge and the power of self-awareness, so it is essential for successful lucid dreaming. If you enter your dreamscape with fears and negativity, your experiences will suffer. You need to believe you are capable and worthy of the best the dreamworld can give you.

Many people live in an illusion. They believe in material objects and pursuing happiness through stimulants and unhealthy relationships. They fail to realize that the healthiest relationship you can have is with yourself. They quarrel over the merest thing and allow their emotions to rule their life.

Awareness is like a bright light that illuminates your world. It shines through the darkness and helps you understand why knowledge is the key to happiness. You need to know yourself and the world you live in to become truly self-aware. This quality isn't present from birth and needs to be developed.

You need to become the omnipresent observer to increase your awareness. Spend your days observing other people as well as yourself. Analyze, reflect and consider all aspects before reaching a conclusion and keeping it all in your memory. Some of the greatest writers in history used these types of observations to create complex characters and apply them to novel situations.

When you dream lucidly, you are creating a world that is designed for you. Even though you are the center of this world, you can't control what happens if you are riddled with fears and emotions. You need a lucid mind to dream in a lucid fashion. Awareness is all about knowing how you feel and how your feelings are affected by others.

Consider a common situation when emotions dictate your actions. You are traveling home from work when somebody cuts you up at a junction. You are angry and shocked. Such reckless driving could have killed you. When you arrive home, you are still angry, and you pick an argument with your partner. You are taking out your frustration and anger on somebody else because you can. Now stop and consider why you are doing it.

What do you feel? Are you making yourself feel better by making someone else feel bad? Conflict often arises from emotionally charged events that have nothing to do with the person involved. Can you become aware of your anger and stop it before you affect someone else? That is a sure sign of self-awareness.

Be Aware of Your Body

How does your body feel after exercising? How do you feel in the evening if you have drunk too many cups of coffee during the day? When do you have the most energy? What happens when you have a glass of wine? Do you feel bad the morning after? Your body may be left behind in the bed when you dream, but the sensations you feel will be real. Attuning your mind to physical experiences will help you get the most from your dreaming.

Be Aware of Other People

Do you label people within seconds of meeting them? Do you see something about them that influences that label? Try putting your prejudices aside and treating them as an individual. What do they do, and how do they behave toward you? When you treat people with respect, you start to see the depth of character and a better sense of personality in others.

Listen to other people and evaluate the information they are giving you. Every time you interact with someone, try to take something away from the encounter. Some people will influence you with their strength and make you want to be better while other people won't. Even when you meet someone who isn't successful or hasn't made the most of their talents, you can learn from their shortcomings. Why did they take the path they did, and what can you do to avoid making the same mistakes?

Think of the outside world as a warehouse filled with a rich repository of information. You can get your information free of charge, and at any time you need it. Take advantage of your chances and use them well.

Ditch Social Media

Have you ever noticed how much useless information is on the internet? Click baits and advertisements are filled with misinformation and fake news. Instead of concentrating on these sources of information, seek out your own sources instead. Read books, newspapers, and articles to find out why things happen. Read about subjects that are alien to you instead of concentrating on your normal subjects. Ask searching questions and find out the answers.

What is happening in your environment? What is the political situation in your state? What are the issues affecting your neighborhood? Do you have an opinion on the subject? Make yourself heard and get involved.

Be Alone as Much as You Can

In the modern world, you are rarely alone. When was the last time you were alone with your thoughts? Information is constantly raining down on us like an avalanche. Do you feel uncomfortable in a room without some sort of stimuli? Music, TV, or other people are a constant in modern life, and it can be hard to get "me time." Make time for yourself and break your normal habits. Time alone will help you decipher what you want and how to get it.

If you have been sailing through life being led by fate or the general stream of life, you aren't completely self-aware. You need to improve not just for your lucid dreaming experiences but for life in general. Awareness gives you choices and increases your understanding of the role you play in your destiny.

When you are alone, try listing your ambitions and goals. When you have a plan for your life, other aspects fall into place. Short-term goals can be as simple as you like, while long-term goals should be more detailed.

Here are some examples of both:

Section 3: Lucid Dreaming: The History and Timeline

The scientific community recognized the existence of lucid dreaming in 1978, but the practice has been around for thousands of years. Dreams and their portents have been figured in cultural histories since 1,000 BCE - the term used to denote the time before the Common Era, also referred to as BC or before Christ.

The first textual reference to lucid dreaming appears in the Upanishads, which is the series of treaties and philosophical texts that form the theoretical basis for the Hindu religion. The school of thought contained many references to rituals and levels of consciousness that suggested the existence of an alternate reality that could be accessed through lucid dreaming. The teachings encouraged followers to enter a trance-like state to commune with higher beings and relate their wisdom to others.

Indian philosophers also taught the animistic tract known as the Bonpo. Tibetan shamans practiced ecstasy and ritual magic techniques that worked with energy to enter a dreamlike state and form a healing link with the higher beings. They believed that these links were part of the rejuvenating and enlightenment process that man needs to grow. The term "bon" translates as 'boundlessness" and is a summary of what we all hope to gain from our own lucid dreaming experiences.

Section 4: How to Keep an Accurate Dream Journal

Throughout this book, we will refer to the importance of dream journals, so it is important to get it right. They should be at your bedside, ready for you to record what happened in your sleep.

The Step-by-Step Guide to a Successful Dream Journal

Step 1: Choose a notebook. This should be a smallish, easily accessible book that is solely used for recording your dreams. Don't use it for shopping lists. This is your go-to guide for all your dream experiences, and you shouldn't write stuff in it that does not relate to your dreams. Make sure you have a couple of pens available as well.

Step 2: Create a template for your dream. This is the most important difference between a successful dream journal and a selection of random scribblings.

What to Include in Your Template

- The location: Was it a familiar place or were you somewhere unknown? Was the location an earthly one, or was it a fantastic place that would never occur on Earth?

- How are you feeling? Does your mood change as the dream progresses? Are these feelings intense or normal?

- Who is with you? Are there other people in your dream? Are you visited by a succession of people who have no tangent connections? Are they friends of yours or do you know them from other places? Are they famous or are they relatives of yours that you haven't met?

- The weather: This may seem strange, but the weather conditions will often set a tone for your dream. Wet and windy weather will indicate turbulent emotions, while sunshine and clear skies mean you are happy.

- What are you doing? Are you active during the dream, or are you merely an observer? Can you do magical things, or do you have impossible abilities?

- Dream symbols: What are the main things in your dreams? Is there a particular house or animal that always seems to appear in the most random places? When you notice symbolic items in your dream, it can mean they are sending you a message.

- How do you feel as you take a retrospective view of the dream?

- Title: These can be as descriptive as you like, or they can be one word that distinguishes it from your other dreams.

Step 3: Start to write as soon as you wake up. If you are on a tight schedule because of work or family, make sure you set your alarm ten minutes early. Reaching for your journal should be the first thing you do every morning.

Step 4: Write in the present tense. When you use the past tense, you are already consigning your dream to your memories. The dream journal will help you relive them and get a clearer picture of what happened. Put your mind back in the dream and recount what happens as if it is happening right then.

Step 5: Set your intentions to remember your dream: Before you go to sleep, say, "My dream will be as clear as day, and I will remember it tomorrow morning." These types of affirmations will encourage your brain to take more notice of what happens as you sleep.

Step 6: Make this a daily ritual: Even if you wake up and are running late, you can always spare a moment to recall what happened while you slept. If there are no memories, simply put "No dreams" on the page and carry on.

Step 7: Take it with you: As you leave the house for the day, slip your journal into a bag or keep it in your pocket. If you get a flash of recognition or remember something during the day, you can add it to your account. If you prefer tech options, try one of the dream journal apps available online. The dream journey ultimate app is available on Google Store and is rated 4.4 out of 5.

Step 8: Read other dream journals: Reddit has plenty of examples of dream entries and how you can use them to track your nighttime journeys successfully.

Step 9: Experiment: If writing stuff down is a chore for you, why not try voice messages? Record your memories on your phone and store them in a file so you can look back at the end of the week.

Step 10: Use different mediums: Sketching a scene can be just as helpful as writing the details. Keep a couple of differently colored pens with your journal to give your sketches more depth and detail.

Are you convinced that keeping a dream journal is the best way to recall and enhance your dream experiences? Start today, and you won't look back. Journaling doesn't just help you with your lucid dreams; it is also helpful for your overall feeling of well-being. When we take control, it feels good!

Section 5: Lucid Dreaming Stories

When you are considering lucid dreams and what to expect, it can be difficult to imagine what will happen. When you sleep, you relinquish part of your normal control and enter a world that can be disturbing. Will all your lucid dreams be pleasant, or will you experience unpleasant experiences?

The reality is that you may experience sadness or anxiety, but you have a measure of control that is more effective than when you have a nightmare. Not every lucid dream will be filled with joy and happiness, especially for beginners. Negative emotions will creep in just as they do in real life, but you will be able to deal with them. The best way to understand how lucid dreams will affect you is to listen to stories of other people's lucid dreams and learn first-hand what to expect.

Dream 1: Falling in Love with the Girl in Red

Can you fall in love in a dream? If you can fall in love within seconds in real life, why can't the same apply in a dream state? Lucidity means you will remember the sensation of falling head over heels, and it can trigger you to act in the physical world.

This dream has been published before as an anonymous account of finding love and is a great account of a positive lucid experience.

I'm walking down a quiet high street in the middle of the night. The streetlamps are the only source of illumination, and the streets are dark and deserted. I feel a warm wind at the back of my neck, and I look around and see newspapers blowing in the wind. I remember thinking how strange that was as it had been deadly still all day.

Despite the dark and miserable weather, I am overcome with happiness and joy. I hug myself and begin to walk swiftly down the street. Lights begin to appear on the horizon as households begin to rise and turn on their appliances. The sun appears in the sky and casts a warm glow on my face. I know the sunrise has been accelerated, but I feel like it is just another day.

I hear a singing sound from behind me. Birds are joining in, and the sound is getting louder. Everything is getting brighter, and the sun is high in the sky despite it being five minutes after sunrise. Then I see her—a beautiful girl with the face of an angel and long blonde hair. Small animals are heralding her appearance like in a Disney film, and she smiles. Her look is the catalyst for all of nature to get brighter, and I find that we have changed location.

We are now in a meadow, and all thoughts of the high street are forgotten. Her eyes meet mine, and I feel an explosion in my chest as my heart expands and begins to beat faster/ I look down and see my chest rising with each beat like a character from an animated film. I look at her and notice she is dressed completely in black, yet she shines like a bright light.

As the scene falls away from me (that's me waking up), I now know that love is out there, and I need to find the girl in black. I love her as fiercely as is physically possible, and I know she is waiting for me somewhere.

Dream 2: Dream Food and Shopping

One of the most fun things you can do when you lucid dream is travel to places you have always wanted to visit. This dream was experienced by a woman who lived in Europe yet wanted to visit New York to do some shopping.

The beginning of the dream is quite loud. I find myself on Fifth Avenue in the middle of a crowd, and the traffic is unbelievable. Yellow taxis whizz past as their drivers hang out of the windows and yell at other vehicles. The sound of their horns is like music in my ears.

I can smell steam and hotdogs as my feet begin to follow the stream of pedestrians, and I feel intensely hungry and crave some fried onions. I tell myself that shopping comes first and then I can eat. Suddenly I see the epitome of shopping heaven right in front of me. The doorway to Saks is right in front of me, and I can feel the pull. As I enter the store, I see people smiling at me and tipping their hats, and suddenly, I realize that I am shopping in the 1950s. The ladies are dressed in immaculate suits that are cut from amazingly colorful and expensive cloth. The men are in sharp suits and are impeccably groomed.

Everyone is happy, they are shopping in the best store in town, and their arms are filled with shopping bags. The ladies are trying on different cosmetics and perfumes as their husbands look on indulgently. I can feel the air of entitlement the people have, yet I also sense their sorrow during the War.

The next thing I know is I am suddenly transported downtown. My bags are full of shopping, and I am sitting at a small table in a dingy café listening to beat poets and music. The air is smoky, and the atmosphere is too cool for school. The owner of the café suddenly gets on stage and announces that the next artist is an up-and-coming comic who is set for big things. As the smoke clears, I see Lennie Bruce step in front of the mike and begin his set. The laughter and smoke mingle together to give me a warm fuzzy feeling, and I think I have died and gone to heaven.

My next recollection is that I am sitting in a small café on the banks of the Seine, sipping a delicious glass of red wine as the smell of garlic engulfs me. The waitress then appears with a plate of steaming mussels drenched in white wine and garlic jus. I savor every mouthful and finish the plate with satisfaction. As I lean back in my chair, the scene starts to fade, and I wake up. The taste of garlic and red wine is still on my lips, and I feel full.

The ability to live a perfect day is one of the most compelling reasons to have lucid dreams, and they make up for a lot of less than perfect days in real life.

Battling with Demons

If you have ever played fantasy games, you already know the satisfaction of slaying giant monsters and demons. What if you could bring elements of fantasy into your dreams to make them even more exciting? This experience did exactly that:

Section 7: Hypnagogic Exercises

Hypnagogia may sound like a weird experience, but you have all had it even if you never paid attention or thought about it before. It is a state of wakefulness between awareness and falling asleep. As you begin to fall asleep, you witness a mesmerizing array of sights and sounds that signal the beginning of your dream state.

As if your eyelids were a movie screen, hypnagogic images will flit across them and provide you with a light show that begins with phosphenes. These vague blobs of light will encroach your vision in the form of purple or green orbs of luminescence that hang around and eventually evolve into geometric shapes and imagery. The darkness of your closed eyelids will soon be filled with faces and landscapes that are accompanied by voices and sounds that complement your visions. Music will often accompany your spectacular field of vision and draw you into the hypnagogic state that can lead to lucid dreaming.

Some people believe that hypnagogia is the brain's way of clearing its junk so we can sleep better, while others believe it is more complex than that. Theories suggest that training the mind to suspend the hypnagogic state is the best way to enter wake-induced sleep. Freezing the mind while experiencing deep hypnagogic levels helps judge the depth of your meditative state and work with it to experience lucid dreaming.

Exercise to Help You Develop Control

Hypnagogic Exercise #1

While hypnagogia occurs naturally as you fall asleep, you can observe the phenomenon while mentally alert and aware. If you haven't been aware of hypnagogia in the past, try this exercise to experience what to expect.

Make yourself comfortable and remove outside stimuli from your environment. Close your eyes and cup your hand so it can cover your eyes without touching your lids. Focus on the distant part of the darkness. What do you see?

Once the glare of the outside world has faded, you should be able to see the phosphenes begin to form. The shapes and lights will form a holographic wallpaper that fills the darkness and creates visual imagery.

Direct your focus to the individual forms of energy and watch as they begin to transform into more substantial geometric shapes. Can you hear anything? Now shift your focus onto the other shapes you see and observe them as they change.

Hypnagogic Exercise #2: Also Known as WILD

This form of lucid dreaming is also known as Wake Induced Lucid Dreaming and involves interacting with your hypnagogic self and entering a lucid dream state on demand.

Stage 1: Relax Into a Corpse Pose

Think about how you fall asleep at night and how natural the process is. You are going to replicate the process with one small difference, your body will fall asleep, but your minds will stay awake. Don't worry if you don't get it the first time, as practice will make it easier. Just because the concept sounds unnatural doesn't mean it isn't possible. Once you master the exercise, it will become one of your natural abilities to slip into your dreamscape while retaining full awareness.

Choose a time when your body is already relaxed and loose. This naturally occurs the following sleep, so the exercise works best when it is done after 4 hours of restful sleep. Lie on your back in the corpse pose and close your eyes. Imagine floating on a cloud as the darkness begins to clear. Get rid of any outside thoughts and silence your inner monologue.

Stage 2: Relax Your Body Completely

Breathe in and hold it for the count of ten. Slowly exhale and repeat ten times. You are now relaxed and ready to begin the exercise. After a short while, you will begin to observe the onset of your hypnagogic state. The colorful phosphorescence will flow across the back of your eyelids and begin to form geometric patterns. Relax and go with the flow as the light show intensifies.

Feel yourself being drawn into a deeper form of relaxation. Interact with your phosphorates and practice forming them into images that will form your dreams. At this stage, you can decide just how much input you want to have in the lucid dream. Do you have an idea of what content you want, or do you prefer to let the hypnagogic images form organically?

Now embrace the other signs you have achieved hypnagogic stature. Music and voices could be accompanied by some physical sensations like floating or being rolled on the bed. Don't worry about these feelings, as they are all part of the experience.

Remember to keep hold of your conscious self and resist the temptation to fall asleep. You need to be aware to experience lucid dreams.

Stage 4: Enter the Dream World

As your internal dream world expands, jump on that cloud and go with it. Let it evolve from the images you are observing and embrace the sensation. As you delve into your dream world, this is the point where you will normally fall asleep. Repeat the mantra "I'm dreaming, I'm dreaming" as your resist the temptation to submit to sleep.

Expect the unexpected at this stage. It's okay to be startled, but don't let your hypnagogia wake you up. You will hear voices, see images and feel sensations that may be familiar or totally alien. Now is the point when you may feel a form of disassociation as your body becomes a distant memory. You are aware of it lying in your bed, but your consciousness has broken free.

Stage 5: Create Your Dreamscape

Now it's time to launch your preferred dream scene.

You will know if the exercise is at the point where you can move forward into a dreamscape. If it isn't, don't worry, you can always try again. Enjoy the light show for a bit longer and let yourself fall asleep. If you are ready, prepare yourself for a wild ride!

There are different methods to launch yourself into your dreamscape, and you need to try them to decide what works for you:

Method 1: Visualization

Picture the scene you want to create. At this point, you will have complete control over the hypnagogia images in your eye-line, and they can be manipulated to make your masterpiece, or you can leave them as they are. Draw a scene that lies way beyond your visual imagery and create a vivid environment that calls to you. Now immerse yourself into the scene and begin to experiment with Kinetic movements. Walking and running can help you form a path to your alternate self and propel you further into the dreamscape.

Once you feel your mind is completely absorbed in your alternate reality, it's time to let go of your physical ties. Let your body fall into a deep sleep and disconnect with it completely. You are still aware of the body below you, but you have no connection with it.

As the moment of complete disassociation occurs, you will feel a shift in your mental state. You will burst into your highly vivid dream world with all your senses alive and popping. You will enter your dream in HD with extraordinarily little effort and find it is fully tangible and interactive.

Congratulations, you are now lucid dreaming, and you have full control over what happens next.

Method 2: The Out of Body Exit

When you are in a hypnagogic state, you can become so caught up in the experience that you neglect to create a dreamscape. If you haven't got a dream scene, where will your awareness be drawn to? The solution is quite simple. Your bedroom becomes your dreamscape, and you are lying in a dream bed within a dream bedroom.

Now look around and distinguish what features are different. There will be some startling changes that will indicate that you are lucid dreaming. Check out your reflection in a mirror, and if the image is blurry or distorted, you are lucid dreaming. Is there a buzzing noise or vibrations accompanying your images? This is a strong indication that you are lucid dreaming.

Your body may feel paralyzed at this stage. Don't panic. This is a normal process your body uses to stop you from injuring yourself. You can break the Antonia by moving a limb or any other part of your body that isn't affected by the paralysis.

At this stage, it's important to remember that you are in a bodily concept that limits your experience. You feel attached to your physical self, which will prevent you from entering a more vivid and attractive dreamscape, so what can you do? Since you are already lucid dreaming, anything is possible, so picture yourself leaving your physical body and moving on to wherever you want your lucid dream to go.

Remember the sensation of swinging above the ground when you were on the swings in the park? The sensation of floating in the water or flying like a bird. These are all ways you can exit your dream bedroom and begin your journey to a new dreamscape. This type of Kinetic sensation should also free you from any form of sleep paralysis or inertia.

Visualize the place you want to be and ask for assistance to get there. If you want company on your journey, just ask for it. This can be whoever you like; after all, this is your experience, so asking for help from Elvis to take you to a tropical beach is perfectly acceptable.

Teleport yourself and any company you have to wherever you like. Spend time at the beach with Elvis before you transport yourself to Jupiter with Kenny from South Park.

Learning this technique is one of the trickiest parts of lucid dreaming. Other techniques are simpler but don't include the intensity that this technique does. The upside is that even failed WILD or hypnagogic exercise can be amazing. Keep trying and enjoy the experience.

Section 8: Mnemonic Induced Lucid Dreaming (MILD)

What is a Mnemonic?

Mnemonics are tools to help you remember things. When faced with large amounts of information, our brains need mnemonics to help us remember the facts and the order that they should be presented.

Common Mnemonics

The order of the planets from the sun, nearest to furthest, has long been difficult for schoolchildren to learn. Using a mnemonic has made it easier

- Mercury
- Venus
- Earth
- Mars
- Jupiter
- Saturn
- Uranus
- Neptune

Kids worldwide will know the phrase "My very excited mother just served us noodles," which represents the order of the planets.

Similarly, the Order of the Great Lakes

- Superior
- Michigan

- Huron

- Erie

- Ontario

"Superman helps everyone" is the mnemonic that represents the order of the lakes. Of course, we know that "every" and "one" should be one word, but there is room for discretion in the world of mnemonics.

So, what do mnemonics do for lucid dreamers?

Lucid dreaming is all about remembering things and immersing themselves in their dreamscape. If you already have a strong recall of your regular dreams, you have a good foundation for lucid dreaming. The MILD technique is centered on the concept of priming your mind to be aware. This means your awareness levels during the day should be at their best, so you carry the ability with you as you sleep.

Now for the good news. This technique is aimed at beginners, and there are no special skills required. Of course, the work you have done to improve your self-awareness will help, and you will soon master this simple technique.

There are four parts to MILD, and two of them can be done right now while the other two will happen just before you go to sleep:

1) Dream recall

2) Reality checks

3) Affirmations for lucidity

4) Dream visualization and setting expectancy levels

Step 1: Remembering Your Dream

If you already have a dream journal, you know how much you remember and have perfected the process of dream recall. If you are new to the process, there is an experiment you can try to test your power of recall. It does involve a real commitment to the experiment for at least one night, but it will give you an indication of what happens when you dream.

Set your alarm to wake you after 4.5 hours of sleep. This is a rough estimation of the end of your first REM sleep pattern. If you are lucky, this will be the point where you have the most vivid recollections of the dream state you have just woken from. Write down what you can remember, and prepare to go back to sleep.

Set your alarm to go off every 90 minutes for the rest of the night. Readjust if you are having trouble falling asleep after each alarm. Make sure you get a full night's sleep, even with the interruptions and periods of wakefulness. Try this experiment at the weekend and limit it to just a couple of nights. You don't want to burn yourself out.

Step 2: Reality Checks

This is where the mnemonics step in. You are testing reality during the day and repeating your actions in your dreamscape. These are known as reality checks.

During the day, set your alarm to go off every hour. When it beeps, try pushing your thumb through your palm. Obviously, nothing happens, and your thumb behaves normally. When you try it within a dream, who knows what will happen? It could go through your palm and end up sticking out of the bottom of your hand.

This is a prompt to trigger introspection, which leads to the realization that you are in a lucid dream.

Here are some easy reality checks for you to perform when you are dreaming:

- How is your breathing? Can you hold your nose and shut your mouth, yet you can still breathe?

- Leap: As you leave the ground, how do you return? Do you float or fly down?

- Read: Are there things to read in your dreamscape? Do they always say the same thing, or do they change every time you read them?

- Vision: How is your vision? Can you see things vividly, or is everything blurred?

- Hands: What are your hands doing? Can they hold things, or can you pass things through them?

- Clocks and watches: Are they telling you the time, or are they behaving weirdly? Watches and clocks behaving strangely are often a sign you have achieved lucidity.

- Traveling: Can you fly or hover to different places? Does the ground disappear below you when you travel?

- Nails: How do your nails look close up? Do they look normal, or are they unusual?

- Reflections: How does your reflection look in a mirror or water? Is it a clear reflection of you, or does it look like someone else?

- Mental arithmetic: Can you perform simple sums? Add together two numbers and see what your answer is.

Do your checks mindfully and use them to reach reason-based conclusions. Be patient and make these checks a part of your regular routine.

Step 3: Affirmations

Just before you go to sleep, go through some lucid affirmations in your mind or out loud. Use whatever works best for you. This is another key stage of the mnemonic effect on your dreams. You are programming your mind to follow instructions and commands that will lead to lucid dreaming.

Repeat the following affirmations or make your own depending on your preferences:

- When I'm dreaming, the images will be vivid, and I will remember them

- The next thing I see will be a dreamscape

- I will have a lucid dream tonight

- I am currently dreaming

- Tonight will be amazing

- My journey will be interesting and fulfilling

Put real feelings into your mantras and believe them. Chant them until you feel yourself falling asleep and stay focused. If you feel other thoughts drifting into your mind, dispel them and keep your affirmations strong.

Step 4: Visualize Your Dream

This is the most enjoyable part of the process. Once you are relaxed and feeling ready to sleep, begin to imagine what will happen next. Focus on your recent dreams and how you would re-live them if you had the chance. Picture the scene in your head and pick up the details you can remember. Focus on one item that will serve as your dream trigger. This can be a person, an object, or a location that features heavily in your dream. The best dream items are things you wouldn't see in real life and feel fantastical.

Say to yourself, "Now I'm dreaming," even though at this point you are just daydreaming. Now imagine what you would do if this were a lucid dream? Would you fly or seek out a character within your dream?

At this point, you will most likely fall asleep, and that's okay. The last thing on your mind was the lucid dream and what you could do if you had one. This is the primary purpose of MILD. Mission accomplished.

At some point, something will happen that will transport you into a lucid state. Your imaginary dreamscape is just a portal to your lucid dreams. You need to practice and believe that your MILD technique will lead to you becoming part of your own lucid dream.

Section 9: How to Get the Best Out of Your Lucid Dreams

When you have mastered all your REM sleep patterns, your dream journal is a regular part of your day, and you have your reality checks in place, you are all set to get the best from your lucid dreams.

When you first start your lucid journeys, it can be difficult to leave the concept of reality behind and the conflicts of the physical world. The experience of outstanding freedom and boundless abilities can be overwhelming. Your dream life bears little comparison to your real life, and that's the point of lucid dreaming. There are no barriers or constricts within your dreamscapes, and the world is your playground.

If you aren't sure where to start and how to make the best of your lucid dreaming experience, here are some of the best ideas to enjoy your newfound powers and abilities. These tips will help you progress and master some of the coolest experiences you will ever have.

The Power of Flight

Since the dawn of civilization, man has dreamed of flying. Breaking free from the bonds of gravity is a dream that many people have and occurs naturally during normal dreams. However, when you lucid dream, you are more aware of the dangers of flying and the restrictions of physical forces.

Your first response will be fear or a lack of belief in your own powers, but once you master the power of flight, you will be able to progress to more magical powers and experiences.

Go for the Direct Approach

If you are courageous enough, just take yourself up to a high building or the nearest tall object and step off. As you fall, open your arms and begin to soar into the sky. Trust that you will fly as opposed to falling, and your faith will propel you into the air.

One factor to consider is your innate fears. If you are afraid of heights, your dreams can play a nasty trick on you and mirror your fear. You could fall to the earth and fail to fly if you don't have enough faith in yourself. This isn't necessarily bad, as it will show you that no harm will come to you even when you fail. Your dreams are a testing ground for your fears and give you the opportunity to conquer your deepest terrors.

Try a Gentler Approach

If you don't see yourself stepping off a high building or leaping from a tower, you can try an alternative method. This is more like a runway method and allows you to build up speed and power before you take to the skies. Find an open space with a clear area where you can run and start running.

Watch the ground beneath your feet fly by as you lean into your run. Increase your speed and feel the wind flow through your hair. Slowly lift one foot into the air quickly, followed by the other and pedal like fury. Cast your arms out to give you more leverage and feel yourself soar into the sky. Feel the exhilarating rush as the ground disappears and you travel through the skies. This is a perfect way to traverse your lucid dreamscape. There's one thing for sure. It beats walking!

Explore Your Lucid Dreamworld

There are many ways to explore your new environment. You can simply give yourself up to the experience and let your subconscious mind take control. This works best when you traverse from a normal dream into a lucid state. Your brain has already set the scene for you, and you are simply stepping into an altered state of mind. Your mind has endless scenarios for you to explore, and you can trust it to give you a rewarding experience.

If you prefer to have a more specific experience, the best way to create it is by doing some research. For instance, if you have always wanted to visit a mountain range and see the views from the summit, you can prepare yourself before you go to bed. Study images or watch a documentary about mountain climbing or exploration. Study the landscape and read up on what the terrain looks like. This will push your mind to create a similar place for you to explore.

Once you have entered your dream, use mantras to raise your expectations. "I'm on my way to the mountaintop" or "Take me to the mountains" will instruct your subconscious to move you through your dream world until you reach your mountain top.

The other alternative is to create a dreamscape that is unlike anything on Earth. Remember, physical constraints don't apply, and you can explore wherever you like. This can be underwater or in space. Visit the deepest chasms of the ocean and explore the secrets of the deep or soar way past the Earth's atmosphere and explore the solar system. Focus on the details, and remember to catalog your experience in your dream journal. These places can be as personal as you like; you can create your own kingdom where you decide everything or visit multiple random places.

Exploring is a really fun way to spend your lucid dream, as you aren't held back by distances or time restraints. You can fly, run, walk or swim to all your chosen destinations and you can decide what happens when you get there.

Indulge Yourself

Imagine if you could visit your favorite store with a limitless credit limit. You could buy whatever you like and indulge your wildest dreams. You can visit a top car showroom and buy the vehicle of your dreams or visit a jewelry store and buy yourself the flashiest diamonds available.

Money is no object, and if you really wanted to push the boundaries, you could even shoplift whatever you want! You may ask what the point is when the things you buy or steal can't come with you to the real world. Just take a moment to consider why you would spend time shopping for things you can't own. The rush of buying something is often better than actual ownership. Indulge yourself with the finest things and enjoy the sensation.

Now take that sensation and find other ways to indulge yourself. Imagine being able to eat whatever you like without outing weight on. You can't overeat or get drunk, so you can eat and drink what you like. You can visit the finest restaurant and sit at the best table in the house. Dine on the finest foods and accompany your meal with a bottle of champagne. Take as long as you like and savor every mouthful.

You can have as many dishes as you like, you won't run out of money, and you will never get full. Concentrate on the food you are eating. Concentrate on the smells and aromas that are coming from each portion. Is it hot or cold? Can you anticipate what it will taste like before it reaches your mouth? When we eat something special in the real world, we take the time to appreciate every morsel, so do the same in your dream world.

Lucid Sex Experiences

Dreams are often considered the perfect place to have romantic encounters and live out your sexual fantasies. There is no danger of emotional entanglements, nasty STI's or unwanted pregnancy. There is no danger of moral repercussions, and you can have as many random sexual encounters as you like. There is one small downside to sex in lucid dreaming. You need to be the initiator as the people you meet will be passive and won't be doing the wooing.

The upside of this situation is that you dictate the tempo of the encounter. If you kiss someone, they will usually kiss you back. If you initiate foreplay, the same response will happen. Like most components of a dream, what happens is based on your expectations. If you enter your dreamscape looking for love yet fearing rejection, you are going to run the risk of being unsuccessful.

These types of dreams shouldn't be seen as the culmination of your sex life. They should be viewed as a bit of consequence-free fun that helps you escape the tricky world of dating. Relax and let the experience flow. Lucid sex dreams are a great place to try out new positions and experiment with your sex life. Remember how you contemplated the food you ate in that fancy restaurant? Do the same with your sexual encounters to get the utmost enjoyment from them. How do you feel? Are you comfortable, or do you feel like you are doing something dangerous and stimulating?

The main thing to remember is you are there for the parts you enjoy, and achieving the ultimate climax isn't your aim. Chances are the levels of arousal and excitement will wake you up before you get to "completion," and that's okay. You don't have to worry about leaving your partner wanting in this scenario.

Meet Whoever You Want To

Have you ever dreamed of meeting your favorite celebrity? Are you convinced that you would become friends? What about sports stars? What would you say to your favorite ballplayer if you ever met them? In real life, meetings like this happen very rarely, and when you do meet your hero's most people freeze and aren't able to say a word.

Lucid dreaming gives you the chance to meet whoever you like. Alive, dead, famous, or fictional, the choice is yours. Imagine being able to meet Sherlock Holmes and becoming his sidekick? What about meeting Pele and playing soccer for Brazil? Anything and everything is possible.

Here's How to Prep for Your Dreamy Encounter

1) Familiarize yourself with the person you want to meet. What will they sound like, or what will they be wearing? Do they look the same up close, or will they be more or less attractive? What will they smell like?

2) Create a 3D model of them. Mold the details you have discovered into a real person. If you have only seen images of these people in 2D, make them come alive. Give them the power of movement and a personality.

3) Set the scene. Where will you be when you meet them? On a film set or in a social setting? Will, you already be acquainted, or will you have to introduce yourself and explain who you are? Will you be yourself, or will you adopt a persona?

4) Make your story realistic. Give your perceived meeting a timeline. Imagine how it will play out in real-time before you enter your lucid dream state. That way, you have a plan if you find yourself floundering. Of course, lucid dreaming could have other plans for you and take you down another route which is fine. All experiences are welcome!

5) Try combining your celebrity meeting with your sexual fantasies for a truly unforgettable night.

Embrace the Magic of Dreams

Have you ever watched a movie and wished you had the powers of the characters on screen? Gandalf perhaps or Bran from the Game of Thrones. The good news is you can have whatever power you like. Dreams operate on expectations, but they also improve as you get better with practice.

Step 1: Begin with a character you love. How do they perform their magic? Do they have a wand, or do they use their hands to cast spells?

What words do they speak, or do they perform their magic in silence?

Step 2: Once you are in your lucid dream, pick an object to practice your magic on. See if you can levitate a pencil or manipulate a bowl of water to form a whirlpool. Cast a spell on a piece of clothing and make it dance around. Use the methods your chosen character uses and retain an expectation of success.

Whatever you try in your lucid dreams, remember to have fun with it. Practice, and you will get better. You will only succeed if you believe you can. You have the mental capacity for these and many more experiences, and the only barrier to your achieving them is yourself.

Section 10: Lucid Tech

Once you have mastered your lucid techniques and are enjoying your dreams, the next step for many people in the world of tech, in the 21st century, we have the tech to turn on or household items, control our heating, and even drive our cars. Everywhere we turn, there is tech surrounding us. Lucid dreaming is no different, and the choices are vast. Lucid tech is growing, and the masks, devices, and machines that you can wear are readily available.

These types of devices aren't designed to make you have lucid dreams; there isn't any form of tech out there that can do that. These devices are meant to enhance your experiences and increase your comfort and the frequency of your dreams.

These are some of the best options currently on the market:

The Remee Dream Mask

At first sight, the Remee dream mask looks just like a regular sleep mask, but the difference is the small rigid patch on the bridge of the nose. This is the brain of the mask. A small circuit board controls the batteries, lights, and sensors that allow you to control your lucid dreams. The settings are controlled via the computer screen. You input the settings you require, hold the mask in front of the screen so the settings can be transmitted to the mask. This neat way of controlling your settings means there is no need for a cord or corresponding port. This makes the mask a great option for mobile use.

The mask works with your regular sleep patterns and is a powerful tool if you already know when you enter your REM sleep phases. The device will set off light sensors to trigger your brain to enter lucidity at the premium stage of your sleep. If the lights go off and you aren't in REM, the device will automatically wake you up. It takes a lot of practice to get the settings right, but the mask is a powerful aid to lucid dreaming when you do. Prices are between $75 and $95.

The Go to Sleep Mask

The technology contained in this mask is more developed, and it replaces flashing lights with a more subtle form of illumination. The tech simulates the natural light of sunrise and sunset to mark the beginning and end of your sleep. There is also a pulsing light to make you fall asleep quicker as it calms your mind and induces a semi-hypnotic state of mind. This light ensures you reach REM sleep quicker than you do when you fall asleep naturally. Priced at $100, this is a comfortable sleep mask that comes with a handy traveling case that prevents damage.

Care for something way cooler?

Section 1: The History of ESP

ESP or extrasensory perception is also known as the sixth sense or esper. It involves going beyond the traditional five human senses to gain information. This doesn't mean you abandon the regular senses of sight, hearing, smell, taste, and touch. In fact, ESP will help you heighten them and use them in conjunction with an alternate reality.

The term ESP was first used in 1870 by celebrated anthropologist Sir Richard Burton. The phenomenon has been around for centuries and has attracted attention and interest since Biblical times.

There were early tests on individuals, but the results were sporadic at best. The researchers centered their studies on self-proclaimed mediums and psychics and were restricted to unsuitable environments. The researchers were more interested in destroying the reputations of the subjects than learning anything from the experiences. They bombarded these so-called sensitives with a barrage of questions designed to expose their trickery rather than their genuine abilities.

Some of the subjects stood up to the questioning better than others, and this was how their credibility was judged. Who knows how many reputable mediums and psychics were dismissed because they didn't have the verbal skills to answer the researchers' interrogations?

ESP made a reappearance in the early 20th century as the German ophthalmologist used it to describe the psychological disorder that led to patients lacking the ability to control their emotions, leading to aggressive and antisocial behavior. He coined the phrase "externalizing of sensitivity" and classed it as a form of ESP.

The term then crossed the pond and emerged in the USA. Celebrated anthropologist and parapsychologist J. B. Rhine popularized the term to cover psychic phenomenon. He became the first parapsychologist to take his studies to the laboratory and conduct formal tests.

J. B. Rhine changed the way people thought about ESP with his experiments at Duke University in 1930. He devised a series of cards with five separate images that are now referred to as ESP cards.

The symbols were printed in stark black ink on white cards that resembled standard playing cards.

The Symbols

- A square
- A circle
- A plus sign
- A pentagram or five-pointed star
- Three wavy lines

Rhine took 25 ESP cards and shuffled them so the order couldn't be guessed. He then asked his subject what symbol was on the card that only he could see. The mathematics and chance factor meant the subject had a 1 in 5 chance of getting it right, and Rhine argued that the subjects that scored high success rates would only happen every thousand times. He also had students that scored extra-chance results that exceeded chance by 1 in a million.

His experiments were gaining notoriety and soon attracted criticism from his peers. The first two criticisms were dismissed immediately

- The statistics were defective: This claim was refuted by the president of the Mathematical Association
- ESP is physically impossible, so the experiments can't be true

Other criticisms were taken on board by Rhine, and he used them to improve his tests.

Some people suggested that the cards were defective, and the symbols could be seen when the light shone on the card. Rhine introduced a form of shielding that meant the cards were impossible to see, even in the strongest form of lighting.

Some suggested that people working in the lab were so determined that ESP was real that they would signal the correct answer to the subject. Rhine dismissed these criticisms and stated that only the main examiner knew the target.

It was suggested that because they celebrated the successes more than the failures that inconsistency in recording numbers may occur. Rhine developed a machine to count the hits and misses so human error didn't affect the statistics.

These tests also uncovered an unseen type of ESP that baffled the researchers. They found that some subjects scored much lower than chance suggested because they were trying to fail. Some people were so disturbed by their ESP abilities they would deliberately answer with the wrong answer to convince the researchers they didn't have any ability whatsoever. What actually happened is that they uncovered a form of ESP that they labeled reverse-ESP, which is just as compelling as positive results.

What Do We Believe About ESP Today?

Western scientists are currently working with Eastern mystical cultures to link the forces that exist in the physical world and those in the extrasensory realm. Research in quantum physics has discovered an epistemic relationship between the confines of reality and the realms of the unseen. Put simply, scientists are now more receptive to the idea of psychic powers and the reality of ESP.

Another influential Rhine was Louisa E. Rhine, a celebrated American botanist who proposed the idea that ESP is housed in a separate storehouse of the mind. Here we find a separate batch of memories, hopes, and fears. Within this storehouse, there was a vast repository of accumulated experiences from the collective experiences of humanity. Think of it as a family bible for the whole of mankind.

The psychiatrist Jung expanded on this theory and suggested that using our natural ESP talents, we can all tap into this repository at will. We simply must master the subliminal psychic access to this repository to benefit from this collective wisdom.

Other theories suggest that all humans have two separate levels of subconsciousness. The second one is classed as the soul, the id, the ego, or the subliminal form of your inner self. Wherever you look, there will be alternative terms for this form of subconsciousness, but the idea is still the same. ESP occurs when the subject actively encourages integration between the two realities and breaks down the barriers of convention.

At this point, we begin to understand the power of dreams. When we sleep, we let go of previous prejudices and enter a realm where anything is possible. The distortions and barriers we encounter in the physical realm are lowered and dismissed. Most people who have psychic abilities will tell you that the first indication they had abilities manifested in their dreams. They began to receive messages that were so vivid and clear that they began to act on them.

Do you believe in psychic or ESP abilities? According to a poll conducted by CBS News, the majority of Americans do believe this. The figures do change depending on location and age, but the results speak for themselves. The demographic map may differ, but around 70% of people believe that these abilities are real. You may believe that others have these abilities, but that you don't. The truth is we all have some form of psychic ability, but we may not know how to develop it. This section of the book is all about finding out if you have the power to use ESP and what to do next.

Section 2: Signs That You Have ESP

During the following sections of this book, we will study the significant signs that indicate individual abilities relating to different forms of ESP. This section is a more general overview of the indications an individual has extrasensory perception. These are powers outside of our normal five senses and are a sign of our evolving and ascending race.

Sign 1: You Have Heightened Intuition

Are you great at reading future timelines and predicting what will happen? You instinctively know what is going to happen in the future, and these feelings come naturally. Do you receive mental images in your dreams about what will happen, or do you get flashes of inspiration when you are awake? These are signs of ESP and a natural indication of your abilities.

Sign 2: You Always Know the Best Thing to Do

When you have a decision to make, do you generally make the right choice? This type of direction arises from the subconscious and combines with the logical part of the mind to form a successful conclusion. What guides you on your path through life? If you have ever trusted your gut rather than external influences, you know you have ESP.

Sign 3: You Know What Someone Is About to Tell You

Have you ever said to someone, "I knew you were going to say that," or do images pop into your mind that someone then verbalizes? This is an innate ability to pick up on energy from others and translate it into a message. Try writing down your experiences every time this happens. You may be surprised just how often you can pre-guess a conversation.

Sign 4: You Know Something Is Wrong

When we share emotions with people, we automatically form bonds that go beyond the physical realm. These types of connections aren't governed by distance, and we instinctively know when something is wrong. There are countless tales of parents, siblings, and friends who have known when someone is in trouble. There are tales of parents waking in the night at the exact time their child has been involved in an accident. Nobody can explain why these feelings happen. They simply reinforce the existence of psychic bonds and emotional attachments between people.

Sign 5: Sense a Presence

Have you ever felt like you are being watched, but the sensation isn't troubling? The feeling is more comforting, and you get a sense of being protected and watched over. This is a sure sign you are aware of the presence of your spiritual guides as they draw near and offer assistance. The thin veil between the two worlds is being penetrated, and you can feel the comforting presence of spirits of loved ones and beings that exist in this other dimension.

Sign 6: You Can Read a Room

Do you walk into a building or a room and immediately sense what the mood is? Despite the environment, you can sense the atmosphere and be affected by it. This means that you can walk into the most run-down messy place ever and immediately feel the joy that the room contains. Or you may walk into a light and bright room filled with luxury and comfort, yet you sense a dark atmosphere that creeps you out. You have a gift for reading the energies that surround you and draw your own conclusions.

Sign 7: You Are a Natural Empath

Do you pick up on people's emotions even when you're trying to remain neutral? Some people encounter a barrage of emotions as they pass through a crowd. It's as if they have an emotional Bluetooth receiver that they can't turn off. When a friend is hurting or grieving, do you feel their pain as if it were your own? Does other people's joy fill you with happiness above and beyond normal levels? Empathy can be exhausting, but it does make us better people.

Sign 8: You Take Trips as You Rest

When you close your eyes for a short power nap, what happens? Do you jolt awake ten minutes later and feel refreshed but have no memory of anything happening? Or do you wake with vivid memories of a mental trip to spectacular vistas filled with breathtaking views and amazing examples of nature's majesty? Do you travel through space and time to visit places that seem alien and undiscovered? Have you ever traveled back or forward in time and encountered people from the past or the future? How your brain reacts when you rest is a sure sign of psychic ability, and these types of trips and visions could indicate the ability to perform remote viewing.

Sign 9: You Know What Is Good and Bad for You

Have you ever picked up an item in the store that looks healthy, but your subconsciousness tells you otherwise? A quick look at the back of the packet confirms your fears, and the product is full of e-numbers and additives. Do you instinctively know what shampoo will be best for you because it includes natural ingredients that suit your skin? This type of intuition will also alert you to natural ingredients that aren't suited for you. Perhaps you have allergies, and your extrasensory perception is giving you the warning to resist this product.

Sign 10: Audio Messages

Do you have inner monologues with yourself when you have a problem to solve? What if the other voice isn't you? What if your inner voices come from the spirit world and are there to guide you? Hearing voices can be disturbing and make you think you are losing it, but they can also signal spiritual messaging. If you don't like this form of communication, simply ask the spirits to tone it down! They won't be offended but they will choose another method of communication instead.

Sign 11: You Understand Synchronicities

Have you ever changed your mind because something you saw triggered a response? Do you have a lucky sign or signal that makes you think again? Do you see butterflies as a sign you are on the right path, or can a lucky number influence your decisions? Coincidences seem to crop up daily, and you feel like a pattern is forming throughout your day. These are gentle nudges from another realm to sway your thought patterns and lead you down the right path. Follow your instincts and embrace these celestial signs as an indication that you have ESP abilities.

Sign 12: You Understand When Something or Someone Is Unwell

When you experience energy flow between all living things, you will also experience when something isn't right with their physical condition. You sense blockages and discrepancies in the health of their energy that can often be specific to the part of the body that is sick. You may know before they do that there is a problem, and you can advise them to see a doctor.

This type of intuition isn't just about physical beings and encounters. If you care about the Earth and the damage that we are inflicting on it, this is a sign you are instinctively feeling its pain. Ecological matters and issues will feel as if they are happening to you, and you will do everything you can to solve them. The natural empath in you will sense illness and bad energy in those around you.

Sign 13: You Have The Urge to Heal

The natural response to sign 12 is to want to help. You need to feel like you are part of the healing process and not just part of the problem. If you feel drawn to medical professions or the services, you are fulfilling your need to heal others. If you study holistic diets and wellbeing courses, you are eager to help others in this way. Maybe you work in the mental health sector and use your skills to heal other people from the inside. Whatever your specific field, the ability to sense when something is wrong and know how to heal it is part of your natural makeup.

Sign 14: You Can See or Sense Auras

Does everything in nature appear to you with color or shade? When you look at someone, are they surrounded by a halo of energy? Sensing auras may seem like the most natural thing in the world if you have seen them since childhood. Most people think they are a natural phenomenon that everybody sees, whereas the truth is they are one of the most powerful signs of psychic abilities. When you see auras, you have a heightened sense of perception which means you are more likely to have extrasensory perception skills.

Sign 15: You Prefer Nature to Cityscapes

When you are in a town or city, do you feel overwhelmed and under assault from your senses? Most of us become more aware of all our regular senses when we are in a busy atmosphere so imagine what it's like for people with ESP abilities. They have at least one extra sense, which means they are at least 20% more affected by noise and confusion. The truth is that most people with ESP abilities have at least two or more extra senses and can feel overwhelmed by the overflow of information they are experiencing.

Natural landscapes help our senses to recover from the cacophony of modern life. The natural, free lowing energies are more soothing and seek to reenergize us rather than drain us. If you feel positive and rejuvenated whenever you connect with nature, your ESP is sending you the signs of what you need.

The bottom line must be that we all have some abilities within, and it's up to you to decide if you want to pursue them. You may be happy to let your ESP abilities occur organically, or you could strengthen them and explore the psychic world more thoroughly.

Section 3: Clairaudience

Translated from the French, this form of extrasensory perception means "clear hearing." It involves receiving messages from sources beyond our ordinary senses. The messages will come from those who have passed from beyond this realm and will contain information and wisdom from spirit guides. Spirit animals and otherworldly energies will choose this method to send their messages to earthbound clairaudients and share their wisdom and advice.

The sounds will differ depending on the message content. They may appear as voices heard by the clairaudient and nobody else, or they may take the form of nature sounds. Some practitioners hear music and others report white noise akin to static. The form of the dialogue may change, but the meanings remain clear. The key to becoming a successful clairaudient is to understand what the universe is telling you.

Everyone has some degree of clairaudience even though they don't realize it. As with any skill, you will improve your abilities with practice.

9 Signs That You Are Clairaudient

1) You hear your own name when there is nobody else in the room.

This form of ESP isn't always a clear voice ringing in your ear. It may be a whisper coming from the corner of the room or voices echoing from beyond your current dimension. You may hear a sentence but may be unable to decipher the actual words or meaning.

2) You enjoy the quiet.

Do you get exasperated in crowded places? Does the noise of other people speaking sound like a cacophony in your head that exhausts you? Loud music and constant noise overwhelm you, and you prefer quiet locations with no disturbances. Natural clairaudients are sensitive to noise and will often shun company to seek a place to recharge in silence. This trait is often attributed to introverts, but clairaudients also experience them.

If you find it impossible to think in loud environments, try noise-canceling headphones or meditation to help you relax.

3) You had imaginary friends as a child

Did you know that spirits will often communicate with adolescents as they are more open to messages? They haven't developed the cynical attitude that adults have, and the spirits recognize their approachability. While adults insist that imaginary friends are restricted to childhood, it doesn't mean the messages weren't real. If you had imaginary friends when you were a child, it could mean you have already experienced spiritual manifestation, and you can reopen those channels again.

4) You love music.

Most people enjoy music as part of their regular lives and will happily listen for a while. If you prefer music to any other form of entertainment, you have clairaudient abilities. Your love for music is a clear way for you to connect with your psychic self and receive messages from beyond.

Your love for music won't be restricted to listening to other people's songs and lyrics. You may write your own songs and hear them clearly in your imagination before you commit them to paper.

Clairaudients can often play instruments without looking at sheet music or having formal training. If you feel deep emotions when you hear music and hear hidden messages, this is a sign of clairaudience.

5) You are a source of wisdom.

Do you have a reputation for giving great advice? How many times have strangers approached you in the street asking for help or directions to somewhere? You have an air of authority and knowledge that exudes from your aura. People just know you will give sage advice and measured responses to their questions, so they feel safe asking for your help.

Your clairaudient abilities mean that you automatically tune into the higher beings who use your skills to channel their messages as you listen to others. Don't worry if your physical self doesn't hear these messages from beyond as your psychic skills have it covered.

6) You have a ringing in your ears.

If you have ringing in your ears, it can be a sign of medical conditions, but it could indicate a manifestation from the spirit world if you have ruled out this possibility. Gentle buzzing or ringing will alert you to the messages you are about to hear. The spirits will often use the sounds to make your ears pop to get your attention. If your ears are reacting this way, it could be a warning from your guides.

7) You are an auditory learner.

Some people have a photographic memory and only have to see something once to remember it. If you have a similar ability with things, you hear it is a clear sign of clairaudient skills. If you have a skill for remembering conversations or prefer listening to audiobooks rather than reading visually, you have developed a strong sense of audial perception.

8) You have a developed sense of hearing.

When you are in a room, do you often hear sounds from the next room that no one else has heard? Can you hear a car alarm going off three blocks away? You may just have a good sense of hearing, or you could be noise-sensitive. This goes beyond excellent hearing and often involves you being aware of the most subtle noises around you. Have you ever looked at a fly on the window and heard its legs tapping on the glass? That's a clear sign of noise sensitivity.

9) You have conversations with yourself.

This doesn't necessarily involve verbal conversations with yourself. This form of conversation is more likely to be an inner voice in your head that forms two opinions and is capable of lucid reasoning without exterior influences. Your spirit guide will guide your inner conversation to include helpful guidance when they feel you need their input.

It's important to understand the difference between spirit communications and internal self-talk. The spirits will never use harsh words or criticism in their messages, and if you are experiencing negativity, it comes from yourself.

How to Develop Your Ability to Communicate Using Clairaudience

Clear hearing can be tricky when outside influences are interfering with your hearing. Practicing these simple tips will help you develop your skills and allow messages from the spirit world to become clearer.

Listening

How many times have you stopped what you are doing and concentrated on what you can hear? We tend to trust visual images rather than audio input, so becoming attuned to the sounds around you can prove tricky. Mastering this practice will help you tune out physical sounds and separate them from spiritual noises.

- Stand still and close your eyes as you listen to the sounds that surround you.

- Pick individual noises and practice listening to them as individual sounds.

- Separate the noises and practice turning the volume up as you listen to them. Imagine you are a conductor with a baton, and you control the volume and appearance of the sounds around you.

Asking Questions

Your initial request is an important part of the answer you receive. If you ask questions that are too detailed, you run the risk of misinterpreting the answers you are given. Concentrate on advice and guidance and form requests rather than demands. Communicating with spirits should be based on emotions and inner feelings. Attuning your body to receive answers is a key part of the process, as is asking the correct questions.

Strengthen Your Fifth Chakra

Your fifth, also known as your throat chakra, represents communication and is the heart of clairaudience skills. Strengthening this chakra will help you receive your messages in their purest form.

- **Surround yourself with blue**: Every chakra has a representative color, and blue is associated with the fifth. Wearing blue clothes or accessories help you tune in and connect with your throat. Use bright blue artwork to inspire you to work on your connections in the home.

- **Crystals:** As with colors, certain crystals work best with the fifth chakra. Blue appetite, lapis lazuli, and shungite are just a few of the crystals you can use to improve your connections. Wear them as jewelry or place them in important parts of your home.

- **Singing**: Even if you don't have a particularly pleasant singing voice, belting out a tune will help you open your throat chakra. Do it regularly and feel your voice gain strength as you improve the communication skills associated with your fifth chakra.

- **Meditation:** If you already know the power of meditation, you will understand the peace of mind it brings. There are no rights and wrongs with meditation, so choose the style that suits your situation. As you achieve a meditative state, concentrate on your audial influences. This will help you improve your clairaudience and your receptive ability to connect with the universe.

Section 5: Mediums

When you think of mediums, most people think of a person who can communicate with the dead. They often seek help from mediums to connect with relatives and friends who have passed into the spirit world. A wider definition of mediums is any person who channels energy through themselves and into the physical plane.

Most mediums seek to connect with energies that are wiser and filled with love. They connect in different ways, but the four most common types of medium are described below:

1) **Spiritual mediums**: These are people who are blessed with multiple forms of psychic abilities. They interact with spirits by visual and audio messages combined with spontaneous knowledge and the ability to sense emotions and feelings. They will often use physical divination tools like tarot cards or angel cards to translate these messages. Some spiritual mediums will use the traditional crystal ball, while some prefer more modern methods like free writing.

2) **Physical mediumship**: Some of the most iconic images of mediums includes physical phenomenon. They show the medium's face and voice changing and undergoing levitation or other forms of apporting. Physical mediums will work with the spirit world to create a physical phenomenon to get their message across. Table tipping and ectoplasm may be accompanied by smoke and loud noises. There is nothing subtle about physical mediumship, and the results can be spectacular.

3) **Healing mediumship**: In Pentecostal terms, this form of mediumship is known as "laying on of hands." The energy of the spirit world is used to heal yourself and others. Some of these therapies are based on indigenous practices, while others have more modern roots. Shamanism is a tried and tested method of healing that

originated in tribal communities and was introduced to Europe in the late 17th Century.

4) **Reiki** is another form of healing that originated in Japan and involved opening the healing chakra to direct healing energies to those who need it. Reiki is a practice that can be taught, and reiki masters will help you develop your spiritual vibrations. Imagine a faucet that originates in your chakras and is suddenly turned on to allow healing energy to flow from your inner being. Once you are attuned to the powers you have, you can turn your spiritual faucet on and off to suit your needs.

5) **Channeling mediumship**: Much like spiritual mediumship, the practitioner will connect with the spirit world and deliver their messages. The difference is they use established sources as a gateway to the astral plane. Channeling mediums will call upon their personal spirit guide(s) to help them contact other individuals who have passed away. This form of mediumship can produce results quicker than a spiritual medium as spirits are accustomed to connecting with new spirits and helping them communicate.

All forms of mediumship involve sensitivity to the presence of spirits. These four common kinds of mediums may seem different to the way you feel your connection, but that doesn't mean you aren't a medium. It just means you fall into a unique group.

Mediumship has come a long way in popular culture. Gone are the images of gypsy ladies in brightly colored clothes asking you to cross their palms with silver. The 1990s saw an increase in interest with the release of the films Ghost and the Sixth Sense. The increase in popularity has led to a growing interest in what it takes to become a medium.

The truth is that most people have natural mediumistic tendencies, but they have buried them under cynicism and disbelief. Not everybody is a natural medium, but they will have the capacity to learn.

Signs That You Are a Natural Medium

1) You are super sensitive to everything.

If the toxic atmosphere we live in causes havoc with your body, you could be sensitive to the spirit world. Food intolerances and allergies mean you must be careful what you eat. You can only use natural soaps and cosmetics, and your skin reacts to certain chemicals. This type of sensitivity signals your gift, but it is also a challenge in real life. You already know that organic food and filtered water is the only way to keep yourself healthy.

2) You have seen some strange things at night.

Spirits know when a natural medium is around, and they will try to contact them even from an early age. Did you see people in your bedroom or heard voices before you went to bed? Spirits work better at night as we are preparing to rest, so night times will have been eventful, and you probably still have a night light in your bedroom today.

If you ever wake up in the middle of the night for no reason, it could also be a signal someone is trying to get in touch. You may experience a feeling of being watched and feel anxious. Don't worry; the spirits won't harm you; they are merely keeping an eye on you. These types of visitations can be controlled by setting some firm boundaries regarding times and places.

3) You love TV shows about mediums.

What is your go-to TV show when you want entertaining? Do the shows Medium, Ghost Whisperer, and A Gifted Man make a list? Do your favorite comedy shows include the Hulu show Deadbeat or the classic British comedy Marley's Ghost?

People who have medium qualities will often indulge in shows and films that portray this type of activity. So, sit back, watch Poltergeist for the 20th time and celebrate the fact you have skills.

4) You have a history of mediumship.

Did your granny hold court in her kitchen and read people's tea leaves? Did your grandfather or uncle tell you tales about ghosts and other spiritual experiences they had in their youth? Medium skills are often hereditary. If you feel like they may be repressing their natural instincts, try having a chat and see if you can trigger a spiritual awakening.

5) Death doesn't worry you.

Have you always accepted death as part of the natural process of life? Do you work in an industry that involves you dealing with death regularly? If you were drawn to aged care or emergency services as a career, this could signal you have mediumistic qualities. You understand that people need to transition to the spirit world, and you want to be there for them.

Do you find it easy to comfort people even when you are grieving? Are you the family member everyone turns to for support when someone dies? You will automatically know how to guide them through their grieving process.

6) You see things that others don't.

If you have ever seen orbs or white mists when other people are present, it could have been a spirit. Hazy mists and ethereal orbs are a popular way to communicate, and they are telling you they see you. Don't fear these apparitions; they just want you to develop your psychic side so they can communicate more clearly. Sparks and bright lights don't necessarily mean you should get your eyes checked.

7) You experience strong emotions when someone mentions mediums.

Do you feel envy or jealousy when you watch the TV show Medium? Have you ever got a reading from a medium and got the feeling you could do better? Feelings of jealousy and envy are a clear sign you need to follow your instincts and strengthen your psychic bond.

What Do I Do Now?

You've checked all the signs on the list and suddenly realized that you could be a natural medium. Are you happy to remain a gifted natural, or do you want to develop your skills and turn professional? There are multiple paths available to you at this stage. Workshops and courses can help you become more attuned with your skills and develop your connections.

You can learn to become a better listener and understand what it means to become a medium by reading books and articles about the history and practice of mediumship. Visit psychic fairs and talk to mediums who are there. They will be happy to share their experiences and help you along your personal path of spirituality.

There are quite a few to choose from if you want to learn from some of the most famous genuine and legitimate mediums. The mediums listed below have highly respected reputations as practitioners of mediumship, and you can learn a lot from them and their stories.

George Anderson

His website tells us that he is the most tested medium this century has ever seen. He is the only medium who was invited to visit Anne Frank's family in Holland. His extraordinary gift has been used to connect people with their loved ones for decades, and he is believed to be one of the most gifted natural mediums ever. His natural demeanor makes him one of the most approachable figures in the psychic community.

Read his books "Lessons from the Light" and "Walking in the Garden of Souls" for inspiration and guidance.

John Edward

One of the most famous mediums in the world, John Edward is the star of the popular TV show Crossing Over. He describes himself as a beacon for other people to learn from. He conducts his readings in a style we can all relate to. He doesn't use any props or illusions to enhance his connections and prefers to be a no-nonsense type of guy. Visit his website for information that will help you on your journey.

Michelle Whitedove

Officially named as America's number one psychic, this is a super cool lady who has it all. She is a psychic detective as well as a powerful medium. Her intuitive health skills help her perform powerful healing sessions, and she is widely respected in the psychic community.

Theresa Caputo

If you like your mediums sassy and with really big hair, Theresa's your gal. She is a regular gal from NY who has a family she adores, and she just happens to talk to the dead. Her TV show and books are a great source of information about becoming a famous medium. Try reading Good Grief or You Can't Make This Stuff Up for an entertaining glimpse into her life and how her skills have impacted it.

Section 7: Psychometry

Translated from the Greek words for spirit and measure, psychometry is the reading of energies from objects and items that have belonged to people who have passed away. It relies on touch and tangible objects for beginners, but as psychometry skills improve, readings can be obtained from photographs or images alone.

Humans are made from energy, and when we touch things, it leaves an energetic fingerprint. Psychometry is the skill of reading this fingerprint and identifying the energies attached to it. For a real-life example, have you ever written something on the mirror in a steamy bathroom? If you have, you know that as the steam fades, so does the message. Every time your bathroom is steamy, the message will reappear until it is cleaned from the mirror. This is a simple analogy of how psychometry works.

Different objects will give stronger readings than others. Items we have held or used more will contain more of our energy and give better readings. If you know about auras and the field of energy, they represent you will understand how emotions and experiences influence energy. When someone is experiencing trauma or times of joy, their aura will become brighter or easier to read.

The same applies to objects. For instance, a well-worn hat that is part of someone's daily wardrobe will give a better reading than gloves that have only been worn once. Metal objects tend to hold more energy than other materials, and a wedding ring is a perfect item for psychometry.

How Do You Know if You Have Psychometric Abilities?

Just like other forms of ESP, there are specific signs that you have this skill. Empaths are more likely to be the best psychometry readers as they are attuned to emotional energies and are genuinely invested in other people.

- Antique stores and thrift shops make you shudder: When you enter a place filled with used items, do you feel weird? Are you overcome with emotions and can't wait to leave? If you get these vibes from old items, you are susceptible to the object's energies. This is a sure sign you have psychometric abilities.

- You cannot own used items: Even in your first home when most of us rely on used furniture, you had to buy new. Old furniture has no place in your home, and you always buy new. The only items of any age are ones that you have owned since childhood.

- You feel claustrophobic in cluttered spaces: Do you avoid places that are overstocked with items? There is too much energy going on, and you feel bombarded by information in places like that. Do you have certain friends who have over-cluttered homes that you don't like visiting? Psychometric people have homes with clear lines and extraordinarily little clutter.

- You cannot wear old jewelry: Precious jewelry is often loaded with energy from the person who used to wear it. Even your relatives' precious items make you feel like you are uncomfortable wearing their heirlooms.

- Pawnshops: When you enter a pawn shop, all the energy overwhelms you. The despair and sadness associated with the items within a pawn shop make you feel wretched and filled with sorrow. Pawnshops are often the last resort for desperate people, and you feel their pain.

- You are compelled to wash your hands when you have touched used objects: Do you feel grubby when you touch other people's stuff? Can you feel residual energy even when you put the objects down? Constantly washing your hands is a sure sign you have psychometry abilities.

Look back at your childhood and consider how you felt when you visited your elderly relatives. Did you hate sitting on your grandma's old sofa? Did your mom's favorite vase that she inherited from her grandma freak you out? If any of the signs listed above speak to you, chances are you would excel at psychometry.

Psychometry is an important part of training for developing mediumship. Enormously successful mediums understand the depth of information that can be obtained using this method, but they also realize the difference between spiritual messages and the messages they receive from objects. In Britain, a law states the holding of an object while purporting to form a link with the spiritual world is unlawful. It is a direct infringement of the Fraudulent Mediums act that was made lawful in 1951.

When mediums use psychometry, they must put down the object before attempting to contact the spirit world. Information from objects is not connected to the spiritual world as it originates from physical links.

Accomplished mediums will use the vibration from personal objects to form a steppingstone into the spiritual world. When we are alive, the thoughts we project into the world are absorbed by the objects we hold dear and have owned for a long time. Psychometry is a form of replaying these messages and emotions to discover information about the owner. The aim is to build a comprehensive profile of them. What their personality was like and how they lived their life.

The Best Items for Psychometry

Personal items like jewelry, rings, keys, and watches will have the most stored energies. Other items like letters and pictures may prove helpful. The main objective of exercises for beginners is to develop intuitive skills to read the objects' information. Historical artifacts are also filled with energy and could prove interesting to read.

A Basic Exercise for Beginners

When you begin to learn this psychic skill, there are two main exercises to practice. The first involves you performing an individual reading, and the other is a group exercise.

Exercise 1: Solo Readings

- Wash your hands vigorously. They don't have to be sterile, but you should wash away any residual energy that may interfere with your reading

- Warm-up hands by rubbing them together to make them more receptive to energy and create friction

- Test their reception abilities by placing your hands with the palms facing each other. Move them apart until there is a short distance between them, about ½ an inch should be sufficient. Is there a sensation between your palms that feels energized or dense? If there is, you are good to go. If not, create more friction by rubbing them together

- Pick up your selected object and hold it in your hands. Let your fingers feel the vibrations and allow them to flow to your mind. Relax and close your eyes as images and thoughts become apparent.

- Make a mental note of all the sensations you are feeling; what can you smell, see, or hear? What emotions are you picking up?

- Ask pertinent questions about the object. Who owned it, and what was their personality like? Are they still with us, or have they passed away? Are there memories attached to the object that you can share? Can you see an image of them using or wearing the object?

Exercise 2: Group Sessions

If you are lucky enough to know people who are just as interested in psychometry as you are, try this fun group exercise.

- Everyone in the group should bring an object they own that has a specific meaning to them or someone in their family. They should give these objects to a designated group leader before the exercise begins

- Place a table in the center of the room and form a circle around it

- The leader of the group selects an object and places it on the table

- Another member of the group is selected to read the object on the table while another member of the group is responsible for recording what they say

- When it's your turn, don't panic, let your breathing flow and approach the object at your own pace

- When you are ready, pick it up and let the energy flow. Talk about the owner and any information you are picking up, no matter how random or strange you may sound. These types of exercises are all about trusting your first instincts and intuition. You should voice your impressions as soon as you receive them and forget about censoring your answers. Nobody is judging you, and they are all here to learn.

- Now, allow the emotions to wash over you. Do you feel a warm, loving feeling flowing from the object, or is it cold and hard? Ask your intuition questions about the owner of the object. Did they love the company, or were they better in small groups? Did they have a fun-loving and playful side, or were they born worriers? Did people find them humorous, or were they serious and hard to get along with? Listen and voice the replies you get for the group to hear.

- Don't be influenced by the object. You need to let go of visual clues that may influence your answers. If the object is a cheap and cheerful piece, that doesn't mean the owner isn't wealthy or successful. The object could have been a gift from their child or grandchild and holds sentimental value. Expensive objects could belong to someone who has since suffered serious financial woes.

- Remember that psychometry isn't about predictions; it is based on the past. Build a complete character profile of the person. Have fun with your reading, and include any quirks and personality traits you feel are relevant. You won't get another chance to say everything that occurs to you.

- Finish on a positive note. Repeat things you feel have the most relevance and sum up your feelings about the owner. State your case clearly and with belief. Once you have finished your presentation, put the object down and step back.

- The group leader will now invite the object's owner and the member who wrote down their thoughts to approach the table. The member who recorded your thoughts would repeat them and ask the object's owner if they recognized any truth in your reading. Some will be totally wrong, and some will be startlingly accurate.

Don't be disillusioned if your readings don't come through immediately. Like all skills, you will improve with practice. Remember that even the most skeptical scientific minds believe in psychometry. They consider it a natural ability of the human mind, so we can all excel at it in theory. These exercises will help train your mind to read the vibrations attached to objects and decipher the content.

Group sessions and solo exercises will help you train your mind to become a successful psychometric reader. They should also be fun!

Honing your skills is a key part of connecting with the past, and as your skill improves, you will be able to recognize vibrations occurring around you. Reading objects is thrilling as you have no idea what they can reveal to you. Imagine the joy of feeling a connection to a lost loved one as you experience their joy and happiness through a tangible object.

Section 8: Psychic Detectives

Psychometry is often used by psychic detectives when they are solving crimes or tracking down missing persons. They use the personal items of the victims of crime to find out what happened to them or where they are. Some police forces are more skeptical than others when it comes to using psychic detectives, but the cases that have been solved cannot be ignored.

These are some of the more convincing cases where psychic powers and psychometry have played a part in solving the most brutal murder cases.

Maria Scott

Maria Scott went missing, but the police soon lost interest as she worked as a call girl. They figured that she had left town with a client and failed to tell her friends. Seven months after her disappearance, she was found dead in a ditch. Her body was decomposed, but police soon established that she had been stabbed five times.

There were around 30 men named as persons of interest in the murder, but police narrowed it down to one man named Mark Brown. Unfortunately, he had left town, and his whereabouts was a mystery to the authorities.

Four years after the murder, it was assigned a new detective named Jeffrey Little. He enlisted the help of a local psychic named Debbie Malone to help with the case. After studying items that belonged to the victim, she told the detective that Maria had been killed at a local cabin on a farm. The police visited the cabin and found evidence that Maria's body had been at the location and was probably killed there before dumping her where she was found.

The murder weapon was found despite extensive work done, and the psychic gained lots of details of the crime by examining the knife used to kill Maria. She identified the perpetrator as Mark Brown, and the police stepped up their search for him. It later turned out that the suspect had committed suicide shortly after leaving town when Maria disappeared.

Paula Brownv

Sydney, Australia, was the scene of the next crime. Paula was a popular hairdresser who loved to party in the capital, but her disappearance soon raised the alarm among her friends and family. Her distraught fiancé sought help from a local psychic who used a grid map, a plumb line weight, and some of Paula's hair to locate her. The police searched the area indicated by the psychic and found the body less than two kilometers from the exact spot the psychic had indicated.

Although the murder remains unsolved, the police couldn't deny that without psychic help, they would never have found the body.

Irene Hughes

Chicago was home to celebrated psychic detective Irene Hughes until she died in 2012. She helped the police crack some of their most difficult cases using pictures of the victims and items of clothing. Using these methods, she helped the Chicago police with over 2000 cases over 25 years.

Tyson Efird

In Arkansas, in 1991, a 17-year-old boy went missing from his job at a local food store. After a huge manhunt, the authorities were no closer to identifying his whereabouts. His mother turned to celebrated psychic Carol Pate to help find her son. She supplied her with a photo, and Pate immediately felt a strong connection to Tyson. She described scenes of torture and had visions of the boy being abused and sexually assaulted.

She described what the captors looked like and identified a word that would include ridge. Most importantly, she assured his mom that her boy was still alive and that they would find him. Pate led police to a property on Ridge Road, where Tyson was held captive. After six days of being held, Tyson had convinced his captors to let him go. When he was reunited with his parents, he was astonished at just how accurate the description of his kidnapping was.

Two men were subsequently arrested and found guilty of the crime. Pate's part in the discovery of Tyson was important, but it was the reassurances she gave to his family that mattered the most. Her constant belief that Tyson was alive gave his family hope in the darkest hours that surrounded his disappearance.

Alexis Burke

When a 28-year-old mother from Oregon went missing, police immediately suspected her husband John of having a hand in her disappearance. Although he reported her as a missing person three days after she had gone, his actions were suspicious to the officers investigating the case. His reactions weren't consistent with a man whose wife had gone missing.

Despite their suspicions, police were no nearer to finding Alexis, so two months after the case began, the family contacted psychic Laurie McQuary to help with the investigation. Using personal items and a photo of Alexis, she began to tell the story of a marriage plagued by arguments and concerns about their finances. She told the investigators that Alexis was frustrated by John's work ethic and his laziness. She described a scene where John had finally snapped and strangled Alexis before enlisting his brother to help dispose of the body.

When the investigating officers approached John's brother, he agreed to make a deal. He avoided prosecution as an accomplice by showing them where Alexis was buried. John was found guilty of murder and served 13 years in the state penitentiary.

Melanie Uribe

Psychics will often find themselves in a position of suspicion when they approach police forces with information. Etta Louise Smith is a classic example of the police misunderstanding the power of psychic visions and the information they can offer.

Smith was watching the TV news one night and had a vision about one of the stories featured. The report told of a local nurse named Melanie Uribe who had failed to turn up for her shift as a nurse at a local hospital.

Her vision led her to do some investigating of her own. She drove to a canyon near the city of Los Angeles and searched for the body of the missing nurse. A few hours later, she discovered the body of Uribe, naked apart from her white nursing shoes behind a bush.

She flagged down a police car and told them of her discovery before returning home. Later that evening, the police arrived to question her and didn't find her story credible. They arrested Smith, and she spent the next four days in jail on suspicion of murder. Eventually, the real culprits were arrested. Louis Morgan, Spencer Nelson, and an unnamed 17-year-old were convicted and spent time in prison.

Smith sued the LAPD for defamation of character and won a settlement for the distress they caused her.

Section 9: Remote Viewing

This form of ESP is a relatively new concept that gained interest during the Cold War with the Soviet Union. The US government investigated how it could use psychic espionage to gain secrets from its Soviet counterparts. During WWII, Russia had heard rumors that the US had been using psychic communications to improve their naval forces and gain advantage over their opponents.

While the truth of the rumors was never established, the possibility of psychic espionage appealed to the Russian government so much that they founded a psychic training program within their military some decades ago. Once the US government learned of the Soviet's interest, they began their own program back in the 1970s to train members of the CIA to use psychic skills to gain the upper hand.

Initially, the test was designed to disprove the theory of psychic espionage. Nobody wanted it to be true, and Stanford University was given money and resources to dispel the risk that ESP and other related phenomenon posed.

Their first research subject was Ingo Swann, a respected artist, scientist, and confirmed psychic who lived in NY. Swann had already proved his ability to remote view weather patterns in different states and had done some impressive work with the American Society for Psychical Research. He was invited to attend the Stanford Research Institute and undergo some tests.

The first of the tests involved a machine used to detect subatomic particles. This machine was equipped with extremely sensitive detection equipment, yet it was buried five feet below a solid concrete floor. The researchers asked Swann to remote view the shielded machine and try and affect its readings. Every time he was asked to remote view, the readings on the machine deviated significantly from the baseline readings it should have been registering.

Once his skills had been confirmed, the researchers began to expand the program. They placed items in boxes and asked Swann to identify them. Swann responded with incredulity. He told them that since he could remote view any part of the universe, this simple box exercise was trivializing his abilities. The lead researchers decided to take him at his word. They purchased the biggest atlas they could find and tested Swann's ability to describe certain points on all the different continents.

One critic of the program suggested that maybe Swann just memorized parts of the atlas rather than having psychic abilities. They came up with a further system based on random coordinates to view people, events, and structures across the globe. Swann didn't disappoint. His results were just as successful using this random system as they were with the regular atlas.

How Do I Practice Remote Viewing?

Increase Your Sensitivity to Unconscious Information

When you are deciding what is happening in your environment, you take shortcuts. 80% of the information you receive is sensory signals directly to your brain. This is your conscious perception, dictating how you process the signals and determine what is happening around you. In today's busy world, our mind is always trying to get ahead and start to move on to the next situation, so it is inclined to take a guess based on portions of the information it has received.

When you practice remote viewing, your assignment is to describe the more subtle information in your subconscious mind and get your information from this source before your conscious mind interferes.

The first thing to do is recognize what the sensory information in your immediate environment is. Take in the colors and vitality of the objects in your surroundings. Are there sounds attached to these objects? Are they loud or low-pitched? What are the smells you can identify?

Now take another look. What are the subtle tones that lie below the brash outer layers? How does the air around you feel? Is it cold, or is it warm? Do the smells you detect have layers? You may smell coffee brewing, but can you detect the smell of milk or sugar beneath the main sensory effect? Imagine seeing your environment from above. What difference does that make to the information you are receiving.

Move from this state to a higher plane and still your mind. Allow yourself to appreciate every moment and feel every sensation. Can you hear the laugh of a child or feel the sun on your face despite you being in a room alone? Imagine yourself rising from the 3rd dimension and entering a higher plane of existence. Become present in your new dimension and prepare yourself for travel.

Practical Exercises

Once you have mastered the process of conquering conscious perception and increasing your ability to see beyond natural environments, it's time to put your skills to the test. Ask a friend to help you and become your remote viewing assistant. Tell them to gather a series of images from magazines or newspapers and seal them in envelopes. The images should be pasted onto blank white sheets with one image per sheet. The images should be real-world images like buildings, people, or pictures from nature, and they should avoid subjects that will be disturbing or provoke negativity.

Once the images have been sealed in manilla envelopes, ask your assistant to stack them in random order. The top envelope will become your target for each viewing.

Sit down in a comfortable chair and quiet your mind. Make sure there are no distractions like phones or electronic devices in the room. The lighting should be dimmed but not dark, and you should have a pad and paper in your hand. The only people in the room are yourself and your assistant. Take deep breaths until your mind is a blank canvas, and ask your assistant to start the exercise.

Write the date and time at the top of your paper and include any niggling thoughts that may refuse to be banished. Now view the first target. You can do this remotely, or you can hold the envelope in your hand - whichever suits you best.

Describe the general image you are getting from the target. Is it a natural object, or is it a scene? Is it a person, or is it an animal? Is there a sense of water or land associated with your mental image?

Write down everything that enters your head and don't try and second guess yourself. The fainter the impression, the better. Describe the information you receive from all angles and aspects. What can you see, smell or hear? Remote viewing is based on the belief that your subconscious mind knows every detail about the target, and it is doing everything it can to transfer that information to your conscious mind.

There will be a barrage of images and sensory feelings all trying to get through to you. Don't panic. You have all the time in the world. Describe the basics and record visuals, smells, temperatures, and tastes. You will also perceive sizes and patterns that are known as dimensions. Emotional reactions will also affect how you react to the target.

Connect the dots. Take the snippets of information you have and begin to form a picture. Take to the air and imagine the aerial view you can see. Sketch all angles and all the visual clues you can recognize. Add keywords to your sketch and make notes about any final impressions you have.

End the session by writing down the time and a brief summary of what you felt during the experience. Summarize your emotions during the exercise and any change once it has finished. How are you feeling about opening the envelope? Excited or nervous?

Remove the photo from the envelope and see how you did. Examine the colors and shapes within the image and compare them to your notes. You will be surprised at the similarities.

Review and Repeat

If you don't have a successful connection with the image, don't worry, it's all about practicing and improving your technique. The main point of remote viewing is about getting to know yourself and working on your ability to spot subconscious messages. Try again with the remaining envelopes and focus on the fun you are having rather than the accuracy you are achieving. Let go of conventional ideas of success and make it all about the fun!

Are All Remote Viewings the Same?

Most remote viewers enjoy describing geographical locations, events, and activities but are less enthusiastic about viewing people. They feel like viewing human subjects is an intrusion of privacy. The viewing feels too intimate, and they feel like a peeping Tom or a voyeur.

Ethics is a big consideration when viewing people, but it is an ability you need to have. If you plan to work with the authorities to find missing people or identify criminals, you need to hone your people-viewing skills.

Fun Exercises to Concentrate Your Remote Viewing of People

How do you describe people? You may never have thought about it before, but how we describe people is different from how we describe places. Try this exercise:

- Set a timer for 5 minutes

- Sit with a pad and paper and think of a specific person you know

- Describe the person you are thinking of

- Is it your crazy best friend who has nose rings and whose hair is ten different colors?

- Is it that college professor you had who wore tweed jackets and looked like Einstein?

- Write as much as you can before the timer goes off.

This exercise is designed to help you use human descriptors to describe your subject. Because you already know who it is, the pressure is lifted, and you feel more able to concentrate on details.

Cues will help you move on to remote viewing human subjects. They will prompt you to include details you may have overlooked.

- Race. Do they have certain features common to their race, or is their ethnicity harder to define? Do they have mixed-race features, or are they classically part of their racial group?

- Height. How tall are they? Do they have a straight posture, or do they stoop when they stand? Do they tower above other people physically, or are they lost in a crowd?

- Weight. Is their weight proportionate to their build? Are they skinny or lean? Are they bigger above the waist than they are below? What is their actual weight?

- Build. How would you describe their build? Muscly and well built or underdeveloped and puny? Are they comfortable with their physique? Are they proportionate?

- Gender. Is their gender obvious, or do they defy gender stereotypes? Does their gender affect how they dress?

- Ethnicity: Do they embrace their ethnicity? Is it a key part of their look?

- Hair color. Does their hair look natural, or is it obviously dyed? Does it suit them? Do they have different colored roots? Does their facial hair match the hair on their head?

- Eye color. What color are their eyes? Are they bright or dull? Do they have a piercing gaze, or do they avoid eye contact? How close together are their eyebrows?

- Clothing. What are they wearing? Are their shoes appropriate? Do they have any accessories or jewelry that are interesting?

- Activity. What is your subject doing? Are they alone or with others? What emotions are apparent during your viewing?

Try Your New Skills Out With a Friend

Now it's time for the fun part. Ask a friend to help you with your remote viewing and take part in your next exercise. Choose someone you trust, for instance, your friend Paul. Ask them to agree on a time when you will be apart and ask them to make notes about what they are doing. For instance, at 2 pm on Friday, ask Paul to make notes about what he is doing, how he is dressed, and where he is between 2 pm and 2.05 pm.

Now give yourself clear instructions about what is going to happen. Tell yourself that on Friday at 2 pm you will be watching Paul wherever he is and whatever he is doing. Describe your knowledge of the target (Paul) to focus on your intent.

Get Feedback

At 2.30 pm ring Paul and ask him for the details of his activities and clothes. Ask how he felt and where he was. Compare them to your notes and see how successful you were. How did you do? Don't worry if you didn't get anything right. Just chalk it down to experience ad try again.

Remember that self-taught remote viewing is for fun. Enjoy your abilities and keep practicing. If you want to take your skills to another level, there are multiple online courses you can enroll in. If you want to work with the authorities in the future to find missing persons or work on criminal cases, you will need to get the relevant certification.

Think of remote viewing as a mental martial art. Beginners and naturally talented viewers are quite happy to avoid the rigors and disciplines that accompany controlled remote viewing, but if you want to progress, you need formal training. The Remote Viewing College offers a complete overview of the information you need to get the relevant qualifications. They have courses available from accredited teachers, and they provide a comprehensive handbook to accompany studies.

Intuitivespecialists.com is another reputable site that offers tuition and training to master the skill of controlled remote viewing. They use methods developed by Ingo Swann, who we previously mentioned as part of the Stanford Research Institute research, and they teach both individuals and corporations.

These courses encourage us to think outside of the box and become part of the spiritual revolution. Our planet is in trouble, and we all need to lend a hand to heal it. The more people who reconnect with the integral soul of the planet, the quicker it will heal. ESP and becoming connected with each other and the spiritual plane are just one aspect of the survival tool we need to move forward.

Section 10: Retrocognition

Also referred to as post-cognition, this form of ESP is the ability to pick up details of people and places based on their past. The word is derived from its Latin roots and means "backward knowing."

It is a common sight on TV shows when psychics go to a location and feel the presence of people or items that they claim are from the past. The most receptive areas seem to be locations that have been subject to trauma, death, or other significant events that have imprinted on the building.

Because we are all energy-based, retrocognition is thought to be the ability to read those energies and translate them into events and emotions. Traumatic or oft-repeated events will cause a fissure in the environmental energy that can be picked in the future. The psychic is tuning in to that fissure and relating the experience they feel or see. There is no concrete proof that retrocognition is a scientific fact or if it just a trick used by people who want to believe they have psychic power.

Paranormal experts do believe that we all have some form of retrocognition ability, and we have the opportunity to strengthen it. Recognizing your ability could be the first step into developing your retrocognition skills.

Signs That You Have Retrocognition Abilities

Habitual History

If we are all born equal, why do we have certain anomalies in our learning skills? Why do some people find it easier to learn a new language than others? Why are we drawn to certain cultures even though we have never visited their original sources? Habitual history is a sign that you have experienced past lives. If you are drawn to certain professions, it could be a sign that this is what you did in the past.

If your birthplace is in the US yet, you embrace Japanese culture and can speak the language that fueled your interest? Do you feel like you belong when you visit places that are different from your birthplace? Maybe you lived there in a former life.

Vivid Dreams

Dreams are often a sign of ESP abilities, but the content is significant when it comes to identifying what particular ability you have. When your dreams are firmly based on historical events, it means you have lived past lives and are skilled at retrocognition. If you dream of being present at the court of Louis XIV in the 17th century or recall fighting in the Civil War, it could mean you were there.

Dreams leave us a trail of clues to who we were and what we experienced. You may have lived to a grand old age, or you might have been a child who died at an early age. If you suffered traumas in a past life, they will be re-lived through your dreams. Past life experts believe that the mistakes and traumas of our past lives help us live a better life in our current existence. Dreams are meant to remind us to learn from our former incarnations.

Déjà vu

The translation of the words déjà vu means the old familiar feeling. While we have already discussed how this phenomenon is a sign of other forms of ESP, it is mostly indicative when considering the possibility of retrocognition. If you meet someone and you instinctively know their character, maybe you met their former incarnation in a past life.

Some people believe we all have a twin flame or spirit groups that we are destined to meet in all our lives. They carry residual energy that helps us recognize them in their current guise. It isn't just places and people who can trigger feelings of déjà vu. We can get the same emotional tugs from sounds or smells we remember from the past.

You Have a Mature Soul

Despite your physical age, you feel like you are a mature being who has lived many times and has a level of knowledge that exceeds most people. You aren't boastful or condescending; you just know you're more developed than other souls.

Signs That You Are an Old Soul

- You prefer your own company: do you ever get exasperated by other people and their endless chatter? You much prefer being alone, and the thought of a weekend alone without other people interfering is pure heaven.

- You have a thirst for knowledge: You love to get lost in a good book and become part of another world for a while. Tasking online courses are one of your favorite things to do. Learning things is addictive for you and is your favorite way to spend your leisure time.

- You think today's culture is shallow: Dating apps and social media make your blood run cold. Why do people place so much importance on how they are perceived online? What are we doing to help other people and save the planet? You think that "celebrity" is a derogatory term, and we should concentrate on abilities rather than fame.

- You can see beyond people's masks: You have an uncanny talent for spotting fake people. You value genuine people, and you have amazing friends.

- Animals play a huge part in your life: This doesn't mean you go gaga over cute kittens and puppies. Even the less appealing animals deserve love, and you recognize this fact. You will often prefer the company of animals more than people as you love their honesty and purity of spirit.

- You have a rebellious side: Because you have seen how the world has changed through your past incarnations, you also recognize the futility of some rules. This doesn't mean you are amoral; in fact, the truth is you have deep-seated moral values. The difference is you know which rules and laws are superficial and should be ignored. You live your life based on your values and beliefs, not other peoples.

- You are a social introvert: Spending your time in nightclubs and bars just doesn't appeal. If you have a partner, you much prefer charging your energy by spending quality time with them rather than a bunch of people hell-bent on "having a good time."

- The role of coach comes naturally to you: Within your family or friends, you are the natural source of information. They will ask for your advice about love, careers, and other general life situations. This is something you love to do, and you welcome their need for assistance.

- Older people appeal to you: If you hang out with older people or have a partner who is older than you, it means you find youths irritating. Maturity is a quality you love, and you prefer to spend time at a slower pace.

Strange Memories

Do you have recollections that are much stronger than feelings of déjà vu? Have you ever remembered something from your childhood yet when you talk to your parents about it, they have no clue what you are talking about? When you check back in your memories, these strange recollections don't interfere with your regular memories. These may be false memories or simple daydreaming so check out any specific locations or landscapes contained within your memories.

Phobias and Fears

When you consider the most common phobias humans face, it is understandable where they stem from. Why wouldn't you be afraid of sharks or crocodiles? Even phobias concerning spiders and snakes are easily explained; they are dangerous and a bit creepy. When it comes to other phobias, the reasoning behind them is less obvious.

If you have an irrational fear or phobia, it could be because of traumatic events in your former lives. Why would anybody have a fear of the number 13? Why do some people fear cotton wool balls? Fear of water combined with dream visions of drowning could mean you drowned in a previous life, and the fear of water has traveled with you into this existence.

Birthmarks

Many experts on reincarnation believe one of the most compelling forms of evidence of past lives are the physical marks they leave on our body. Scientists and doctors will tell you that your birthmarks were formed in the womb by the position you took or were caused by random pigment changes.

However, when you consider the other signs that you have lived on earth before, you can correlate these events to birthmarks you have. If you remember injuries and wounds from past experiences, look for pink or brown marks representing the hurt you have suffered in a former existence.

Passions

What makes your life feel complete? Music, dancing, art, or sport can all be huge passions, but where does this feeling come from? If your family or friends aren't influencing your decisions or passions, maybe it is a sign you were passionate about the subject in a former life.

True Tales of Retrocognition

James Leininger

In the late 1990s, a young two-year-old boy began talking about aviation to his parents. The family was based in Louisiana and had no ties to the subject and was amazed at the details he knew about planes and how they worked.

By the time James turned 8, he was already having vivid nightmares about being shot down by a plane with a red sun on it. He screamed and pointed to the ceiling as he recalled the event in his dreams. James told his parents he remembered a plane called the Corsair, which had crashed and burned during a war.

His father researched the details his son gave him, discovering that a plane called Corsair had been hit and crashed during the battle of Iwo Jima in 1945.

Annie Moberly and Eleanor Jourdain

In 1901 these two British ladies were well known for their powers of retrocognition. They worked as scholars in a respected school and were adamant they were going to find the location of a private chateau belonging to the ill-fated Queen Marie Antionette. The chateau was well documented, but the location had remained a mystery for centuries.

The pair worked on connecting with the dead Queen's spirit, but what they found was more compelling. They reported that rather than contacting the spirit of the Queen, they had, in fact, interacted with her recollections of the past. Once they had details of the location of the chateau, they visited it and experienced a "time slip." During this experience, they allegedly saw images of the Queen and her entourage interacting with each other.

They documented their experiences in a book named "The Adventure," which was met with much ridicule and speculation. The book was a sensation despite people's disbelief and was rewritten and marketed under anonymous names the next year.

Reddit

Some people have such chilling retrocognition experiences that they prefer to remain anonymous. One story appeared on the popular site

Reddit, the self-proclaimed front page of the internet. The person posting the story told of his vivid dreams of being a serial killer back in the 1940s and '50s. He describes his life living on a deserted farmhouse where he lured his victims before killing them and burying their corpses in the woods.

He describes himself as someone who would never hurt a fly in his current life, but he finds himself missing his old persona. He describes his type of victim as "pretty dark-haired girls," and sometimes obtrusive thoughts of how to capture her will flash into his head whenever he sees a girl who fits the description. He says he has never acted on these thoughts and has come to terms with his thought patterns.

The details of this story are so vague they cannot be checked, but that doesn't mean it isn't true. Just because the guy wasn't caught doesn't mean he didn't exist.

So, what is different between these stories and the TV psychics who claim to receive messages from the past? More cynical minds will point out that today's resources are so comprehensive that any building or event can be researched beforehand. It is so simple to get details of people and places that more modern practitioners must work extra hard to be convincing.

But how dies that explain stories of retrocognition before the technology we have today was available? Surely the possibility that we all live our lives in a cyclical manner that involves various reincarnations explains why we have these abilities? The possibility that every soul who lives is a brand new entity defies the fact that as humans, we progress and become more developed through time. The only way we get better and more developed is by learning from our past existences. Tapping into those memories is a skill and should be developed whenever possible.

How to Develop Your Retrocognition Skills

Keep a Dream Journal

Just like other forms of ESP, your dreams are a gateway to your past lives. Recording details of them will help you understand the messages you are being sent. Making notes about what you see, hear, smell or feel will help you possible research connections in this life.

Know Your Past

Contact your relatives and ask them to tell you their stories. The history of your family is a great way to start researching your roots. Once you have your recollections, begin to visit the places they remember and connect with their memories.

This may be the point when you consider a past life regression session with a trusted hypnosis practitioner. You can try the techniques yourself because, after all, we regress every day. Whenever you retreat to the past to retrieve something, this is a form of regression, even if it was four days or four hours ago.

Meditation can help you regress and experience your childhood again. From there, it is a simple step to go beyond this life and imagine what past lives looked like. Self-regression won't cause you harm, but it can mean you are basing your memories on imagined scenarios. Trained therapists are the best way to find out just how your past lives impact your current ones.

Divination Tools

Tarot cards, pendulums, runes, and tea leaves all qualify as divination tools. The cards are readily available and can be used to ask questions safely about your past. Pendulums are also easy to use and can answer simple questions about your past with a yes or no response. Whatever tool you choose, make sure you are safe. Stay away from Ouija boards and other occult tools.

Join a Group

If you want to talk about your retrocognition methods and develop them, an online group will help. Ask your questions without fear of ridicule and share the members' tips and hints. Groups are a great way to become involved in all other forms of ESP and develop your skills.

Section 11: Telekinesis

What is telekinesis? Put simply, it is the power to move objects with your mind. Practitioners can seemingly move or manipulate physical objects without interacting with them in a physical sense.

There are two types of telekinesis described as Macro-PKare and Micro-PKare. The former effect involves energetic manipulation of objects that are visible to the naked eye. The latter effect is based on smaller-scale movements that researchers have to use statistics to examine. For instance, micro-Pk is used to influence random number generators and computer programs.

Celebrated mediums and psychics perform the more famous examples of Macro-PK. The best way to understand the phenomenon is to study the more notable practitioners from history.

Nina Kulagina

Born in 1926, Kulagina was a Russian-born woman who claimed to have psychic powers. For the last twenty years of her life, she was the subject of academic research in Russia that seemingly proved her abilities, particularly her power of telekinesis.

She was filmed under controlled conditions, and the resulting silent black and white films caused ripples in the psychic research world. They showed images that suggested Kulagina could move objects on a table without physical contact. One of the films showed her separating broken eggs into egg whites and yolks in a saline solution using just her mind.

Her most famous experiment involved a frog floating in a saline solution. Kulagina was instructed to stop the frog's heart from beating without touching the body of the subject. She focused on the frog with a fierce intensity and increased the heartbeat before slowing it down. As the intensity of her energy increased, the frog's heart stopped beating, and it perished.

What Is the Energy Used in Telekinesis?

All forms of ESP involve some form of energy. It can be argued that telekinesis is the most physical form of energetic force as it moves objects and creates visual scenarios. The energy used to perform telekinesis is known as Psi energy and involves the utilization of mental energy. Various forms of Psi energy indicate the presence of telekinetic abilities.

Psi Social Energy

This is all about the "vibes" you get from other people and the energy you send out to others. Social energy isn't associate with the niceties of society or having good manners or behavior. If you possess social energy, it doesn't matter where you are in the world; you will universally embrace the culture and be affected by their "vibes."

When you enter a room, the atmosphere buzzes, and people are naturally drawn to you. This is also described as astral energy or emotional energy, but the term social covers the interactive aspect more collectively.

Chi energy is more concerned with your internal organs, and how you process it depends on intention. The nature of chi energy is evolved from the natural energy that surrounds us. Water and air supplement the vitality we get from our food, and the body turns it into chi energy to make us feel stronger.

While chi energy is described as more internal and psi energy is an external force, they work best when combined. If your chi energy levels are high, you will be able to use your psi energy more effortlessly. You will feel the two energies bouncing off each other and creating a powerful vibration.

How to Practice Telekinesis

This is not an easy process to master, but it is worth the effort. When you train your mind to project energy and move objects, the feeling of satisfaction is out of this world. You will feel a connection to your spiritual energy that could light a room with its joy. No matter what scientific studies say and what debates are raging, the key thing to remember is that anything is possible if you believe you can do it.

Step 1: Choose Your Object to Move

This is quite an obvious forts step, but it can be the point where some people trip up. You need to start small and leave the larger, more impressive objects for later. A feather or a paper tissue are both great examples of a starter object. Imagine your mind is a fully formed human being who is just beginning to work out. Your "pushing arm" is the part of your brain where you find your psi energy and should be gently exercised to make the muscle stronger. Once you have the object sourced, it's time for the fun part!

Step 2: Choose the Location for Your Exercise

You need to choose a room that is free from distractions and has a peaceful calm aura. The table you are using to put your object on should be clear of all other items, and you should have a chair that is upright and placed next to the table.

Step 3: Create a Psi Ball

At this point, you need to choose your method of telekinesis. Will you channel energy through your mind and rely on your inner strength to move the object? Maybe you feel a psi power that emanates from your hands will serve your purpose better? If you choose the psi option, it's time to create a psi ball.

- Feel the energy in your hands and create warmth by rubbing them together

- Call on your inner chi energy to create extra reserves and direct them to your hands

- Practice separating your hands and creating dense energy before clasping them back together

- As your energy grows, craft it into a ball and is ready to propel it towards your chosen object

Step 4: Concentrate

This is the key to your success. If you aren't fully focused, your energy will be interrupted, and the exercise will fail. Channel your psychic power and feel it strengthen as your mind concentrates on the task ahead.

Step 5: Visualize Your Energy

If you have already created a psi ball, your energy will be at your fingertips. If you rely on mental energy, you need to visualize your psychic ball in your head.

Step 6: Become One with Your Object

This may seem a bit out there, but trust me, it's easier than it sounds. Every single object in the world has an energy level, and we all share the experience. Like you meet some people you connect to immediately, others who repel your objects are just the same. You need to develop a sense of connection with your chosen object. Imagine what it feels like and how it is affected by the elements. Feel the energy of your object and form a bond.

Step 7: Move Your Object

Once your energies have merged, it's time to try telekinesis. There are several different ways to do this, and you can try them all to find the most effective one for you:

- Command the object to move with your voice. You can vocalize this, or you can use your mental voice. Be confident and imagine your object moving.

- Use your ball of energy to move the object. You can throw it or roll it towards the item, or you can imagine it falling from above.

- Split the energy contained in your hands and create a force field. Wave your hands at your item, or try holding your hand at the side of it and compelling it to move.

The main thing to remember is you aren't trying to force the movement. You are working in tandem with your object and forming a spiritual bond. The experience should be a satisfying one no matter what the results. It is very unusual to get a positive result from your first try but don't be disheartened by lack of success.

Step 7: Be Patient

This is one of the most frustrating parts of telekinesis. You want to move things with your first try, and if that fails, you will be tempted to give up. Don't lose heart; keep trying, and you will see some progress. Keep practicing, and your object will move.

Step 8: Rest and Repair

Just like any other muscle you have, you can strain it with overuse. Rest and relax between sessions and give your mental abilities time to regather. If you are finding it hard to concentrate, take a rest. Mental exhaustion isn't pleasant, and it can have long-lasting effects if ignored.

Step 9: Keep Records

As with any other type of exercise, you need to track your progress. Use a telekinesis journal to take notes about each session. You should include the date, the object, and the length of time you practiced for.

For example, on January 3rd, a small white feather, 12 pm – 1 pm, resulting in slight movement.

Once you have honed your powers and are starting to see progress, consider expanding your journal. Set up your smartphone to record your session and any possible movement.

Step 10: Experiment with Your Objects

If you are struggling to move flat pieces of paper, try something different. Fold the paper in half and stand it up like a tent, so you have something more visible to concentrate on.

Finally, if you feel you have residual energy in your hands when you finish your session, remember to restore it to the ground. Place your palms on the floor and expel the extra energy to the soil.

If you achieve success with the exercises described above, it's time to develop other areas of telekinesis. Switching up your activities and going the extra mile will soon feel as natural as blinking.

Here are Some Advanced Exercises for You to Try

Create a Psi Wheel

A psi wheel is a lightweight pyramid-shaped piece of paper or tin foil placed on a pointed object to spin easily. You can use various objects to form the base, but the most practical methods involve a cork and a toothpick.

Create the psi wheel by taking a square piece of foil about 6x6 cm. Fold it diagonally and open it up. Fold it the other way and open it up. The folds should form a distinct X shape.

Now turn the foil over and repeat the exercise to strengthen the folds. Pinch the apex of the X shape to form a cap.

Take your cork and place the toothpick in the center so it stands as upright as possible.

Place the foil so it forms a cap on top of the toothpick and can spin freely. Blow on the wheel to test its sensitivity. If your breath makes the wheel come off the base, it's perfect.

Now attempt to make the wheel spin using your psi energy. As you circle the base and raise your hands, the energy forces emitting from you should make the wheel rotate. Cup your hands around the base and concentrate on the force you are generating so the foil will start to move.

Some skeptics will tell you that the heat from your hands will form convection forces that will make the wheelwork. If you want to rule out the chance of outer forces interfering with your experiment, cover the wheel and its base with a glass jar or plastic bowl. This means that any movement generated has come from your psychic power and cannot be dismissed as a force of nature.

Control a Flame

Some ordinary household items are perfect for you to train your telekinetic abilities. An ordinary candle gives you the opportunity to flex your psychic muscle. Light the candle, clear your mind and become one with the flame. Imagine the heat and light at the very center of the flame and how it feels to be that free. Now concentrate on the flickering motion and feel your mind connect with the movement.

Focus on it and manipulate the flame. Make it move to the right and to the left. Make the flame grow brighter and make it diminish. Become the flame and make it move at will. Consider using a soundtrack to make the flame move to the beat of a song or a metronome.

Step It Up a Beat

To keep your mind fresh and interested, you should mix and match your exercise. Start with the simple exercise and progress to a psi wheel. Meditate in between to regain mental strength and progress to some more challenging exercises. Place a pencil on a table and attempt to make it roll. Take a leaf out of Uri Gellers' book and try bending spoons and forks.

The main thing to remember is the biggest obstacle you face is yourself. Losing faith or becoming disillusioned will happen, but you need to get past it. Telekinesis is possible, and you can do it!

Section 12: Telepathy

In the 13th century, the popular poet known as Rumi described telepathy as "The voice that doesn't use words."

Our etheric bodies are all part of a spiderweb of energies that link us to all other beings. There is a sea of energy that engulfs us all and enables us to share information and emotions.

There are three established types of telepathy, and they all operate in different ways.

Part 4: Guided Meditation

Meditation is about letting go and just being, yet some people find it uncomfortable and awkward. Guided meditations will help you overcome these fears and emotions and prepare yourself for further experiences. Begin your journey with a tailored meditation to prepare your mind and body for your preferred form of connecting with the astral plane.

These are Some Guided Meditations to Help You Overcome Common Issues.

The Move from a Safe Place to a Brave Space

Step 1: Find a comfortable place to sit and place your arms by your side in a position that makes you feel safe. Close your eyes or lower your lids until just a small number of light shines through.

Step 2: Feel your breathing process. Take note of the motion of air entering your body, and hold it for 10 seconds. Feel the accordion-like process of expulsion as you breathe out. Repeat until you feel relaxed.

Step 3: Now, return to your natural breathing process and feel the safeness of your space.

Step 4: Hold your hands in a cupping motion and imagine something delicate in your palms. Cradle your precious object and raise your cupped hands to rest in front of your heart. Feel how vulnerable your object feels and what emotions generate from it. How does your heart feel, is it nervous, or do you feel strong and protective?

Step 5: Release the imaginary object from your palms and watch it leave you and enter the real world. Now separate your hands and place your palms over your heart, one on top of the other. Use your palms as a mirror, reflecting how you feel inside and what emotions rule your heart.

Step 6: Feel your self-compassion grow and make you stronger. Repeat in your mind or out loud the following phrase "I am strong, I am brave, and I will be my own protector" until you feel strength flow through your veins.

Step 7: Close your palms and feel the strength in your closed hands. You have a powerful weapon in your possession, and it is primed and ready to go. Lower your nose to your closed palms and inhale the force they contain. Exhale and see the shining light that emanates from your inner self.

Step 8: Encourage your hands to spread their strength. You have the force of bravery inside you, so the energy in your hands can work in other ways. Circle your head with your hands and feel the energy pass through your skull. Bring your hands lower to make your body feel stronger and ready for anything. As you work, repeat your mantra of strength and bravery.

Step 9: Take the time to say goodbye to your negativity and weakness. Mourn their passing and feel yourself heal. Consider all the times you have been hurt by other people's negative energies and let yourself close the wounds. You are strong and brave, and nobody will hurt you like this again. You are a warrior who can face adversity and win.

Step 10: Open your eyes and unfurl your limbs like a cat. As you start to stretch, you will feel like a spiritual giant who can conquer everything you encounter.

Prepare Yourself for Sleep Meditation

This meditation has no definite end. There will be no bells or whistles that signal you are ready for sleep. You may have to go back and repeat certain parts of it until you feel completely relaxed.

Step 1: Lie down on your bed in a comfortable position. Splay your legs to hip-width and place your arms by your side or rest your hands on your stomach.

Step 2: Close your eyes and contemplate your breath. See, it enters your nose and fills your lungs before you picture it exiting your mouth. Feel your chest rise and fall as you take deep breaths and relax.

Step 3: Let your thoughts in. It's normal to have a flood of thoughts enter your mind before you sleep. Your brain recognizes it is the end of the day, and it will try to cram in all the information it has about what has happened and what may happen tomorrow. Don't try and stop the process but limit the amount of time you spend on them. Pick out the thoughts that demand your attention and let the rest go. As you deal with each thought, remember to return to your breathing. Come back and focus on your breath before you return to your thoughts.

Step 4: If you feel yourself getting frustrated or angry with your thoughts, file them away. Picture a strong metal box with the word "thoughts" written on the front. Mentally take your frustrating and angry thoughts and place them in the box. Lock it up and put the key somewhere safe. Come back to your breathing and calm your mind.

Step 5: Shift your focus to your body. Begin with your feet and wiggle your toes. Now rotate your feet and feel how they react to the bed you are lying on. Has the temperature risen while you move? Can you feel the pressure of your heel on the bed?

Step 6: Now, pay attention to your legs. Travel up through your lower limbs and relax the calf muscles before you move on. As you reach your upper legs, let all the tension go and feel the lightness of your limbs.

Step 7: Move your focus to your core. Explore your abdomen and feel the sensation of your lungs filling and emptying. Is there underlying tension in your abdomen? Form a circular path from your abdomen to your chest and relax as your focus spreads through your body.

Step 8: Guide your thoughts to your pelvis. Explore your groin and buttocks for tension and emotional stress. Release the muscles and feel them relax.

Step 9: Concentrate on your back. Tension and stress will often form muscular tightness or pinching in this area, and you need to let them go. Imagine an internal heat that warms your spine and releases the tension held in your back.

Step 10: If you are still awake, return your focus to your breathing. Count each breath and use them as anchors to return your focus. Your mind will try and wander, and you need to reign it in. Keep counting until you fall asleep.

If you are having trouble letting go of troubling thoughts, try this simple breathing practice. It will activate the vagus nerve, the part of the nervous system responsible for calming the body and mind:

- Breathe in slowly to the count of four
- Exhale even slower to the count of eight
- Repeat until you feel troubling thoughts leave your mind

The Loving Kindness Meditation

This meditation focuses on letting go of negative energy and embracing the power of positivity. Let love and compassion become your power and let go of anger and aggression. The process begins with yourself and switches focus to other people in your life.

Step 1: Choose a Mantra That Soothes You

Try something simple that states your intention and is easy to remember

> I choose to be happy and well
>
> May I always feel blessed
>
> May I feel healthy and well
>
> Help me live with ease

Repeat your mantra while seated in a comfortable position with soft music playing in the background. Close your eyes and picture yourself happy and content. Where is your favorite place? Put yourself there and feel the sensations of happiness flood over you. Hear the sounds and smell the aromas that you associate with your special place.

Remember, you don't have to choose actual places. You can resort to fantasy locations. Choose an enchanted forest filled with magical animals that light up when you see them. Imagine birds flying around your head as small rabbits lead you into the woodland. As you walk through the forest, keep repeating your personal mantra.

Step 2: The Benefactor

Now consider who your most constant source of unconditional love is. Is it a member of your family who loves you the most, or do you find that kind of love comes from your pet? Who looks at you with love and never judges you? Think of them as you compose your new mantra.

> May you always be happy and healthy
>
> May you always have happiness in your heart

> I wish only the best for you as you live a long and healthy life filled with joy.
>
> I hope you can live your life with ease

Picture them in your mind as you repeat your mantra and remember all the great times you have had together. Now imagine what you can do to make your time together better and more productive. Are there other people who you feel give you unconditional love? Do the same for them and spread the love.

Step 3: Your Friends

Do you have any regrets when it comes to your friendships? Have you let things slide with some people, and you miss them? Before you reestablish contact, try sending them some love. Take a deep breath and picture them in your head as you recite a loving mantra that will help you reconnect:

> I miss you, and I hope you miss me too
>
> May we both welcome each other with open arms
>
> May all our time apart make us stronger
>
> We can make our friendship stronger as we grow

Step 4: The Neutral Person

Now concentrate on someone who is familiar to you but has no negative or positive impact on your life. This can be the guy who serves you at the gas station or your mailman. It can be the lady you recognize from the local store but have no clue of their name. Create a mantra that gives them love for just being them and recognizing the web of people who form your life. Picture them in their normal environment and imagine yourself in their eye-line. As you catch their attention, repeat your mantra until you feel they have felt your love.

I thank you for your place in my life

May you always be in my environment

I wish you health and happiness

I send you love and joy

Conclusion

Hopefully, the world seems like a much bigger place now. You have the skills to unlock your abilities and visit the realms and planes that are beyond our consciousness. Good luck on your journeys, and remember, travel with love.

www.ingramcontent.com/pod-product-compliance
Lightning Source LLC
Chambersburg PA
CBHW050254120526
44590CB00016B/2340